KIDS WHO RUN AWAY

BY

JOSEPH PALENSKI

Published by
R & E Publishers
P. O. Box 2008
Saratoga, California 95070

Library of Congress Card Catalog Number
83-62298

I.S.B.N.
0-88247-727-7

THIS BOOK IS DEDICATED

TO MY PARENTS

ANNE AND JOE PALENSKI

SPECIAL PEOPLE

WITH SPECIAL STRENGTHS

TABLE OF CONTENTS

                    The Nebulous Character of the
                       Runaway Laws
                    Running Away as a "Negative"
                       Experience
                    The Development of a Runaway
                       Role and "Career"
                    Methodological Notes

                    Historical Comment on Children
                       and Absence
                    The Need For Work
                    The Creation of a Juvenile Court
                    Family Court Routine
                    Psychopathological Understanding
                       of Runaways
                    The Reformists
                    Delinquency Focused Research
                    Legal Non-Intervention Thinking

                    The Manufacturing of a Runaway
                       Role

Concern For Identity
Commitment and Career

The Three Stages of Running Away
  1. The Unsettling Stage
  2. Exploratory Stage
  3. The Routinization Stage
Stages and Interpretations of the
  Court
Ideal Patterns
The Experimenter — Indifferent
  Individuals (Cell 1)
The Novice — Indifferent Individuals
  within the Exploration Stage (Re-
  evaluate) (Cell 2)
The Independent — Indifferent Indi-
  viduals within the Routine Stage
  (Cell 3)
The Friend — Friendship Focused
  Individuals within the Unsettling
  Stage (Cell 4)
The Adventurer — Friendship Focused
  Individuals within the Exploration
  Stage (Cell 5)
The Survivor — Friendship Focused
  Individual within the Routinization
  Stage (Cell 6)
The Street Person — Group Focused
  Individual in Unsettling Stage
  (Cell 7)
The Hustler — Group Focused Indi-
  viduals within the Exploration
  Stage (Cell 8)
The Runaway (Cell 9)

LIST OF TABLES

ACKNOWLEDGEMENT

The completion of this effort was made possible through the assistance of many people. Assistance took many forms, and I am greatly indebted to the many persons who helped.

A note of thanks to my teachers and colleagues who assisted me in clarifying my ideas and provided me helpful insights and criticisms. Especially David Maines, who provided me personal opinions and opened me up to an entirely new avenue of sociological thinking. To Rochelle Kern, Edwin Schur and Irwin Goffman of New York University who provided me with encouragement during the life of the project. To Claus Muller of Hunter College who introduced me to graduate work and Philip Kayal of Seton Hall University, a true colleague and friend. To Howard Schwartz, Al Roberts and Theo Solomon for constant encouragement.

Special thanks to the staff of the New York City Youth Board, especially Bob Latham. To Sergeant Joe Elique of the New York/New Jersey Port Authority Police for guidance in the field. Thanks is especially in order to Marie Infranca, Kathleen Dibble, Kathy Grabowski, Barbara Elliott, Judy Cohen, Dot Gorski, Jamie Weiner and Jim Zielenbach for endless editing work and transcription.

My gratitude also extends to friends past and present who simply make life worthwhile. Kathy and Mike Hogan, Deirdre Shea, Joyce Scott, Joe Infranca, Bobby and Geri Palenski, Ron Gorski, Joe Aponte, Jim Hartman, Vanessa Furtrell, Cristina D'Amato, Janine Enrico, Vicki Maro, John Mathis and John Zalner.

Finally to the young people of New York City and those who think they are young, especially Eddie "College Boy" O'Donnell, Humma Clarke, Mr. Jazz 'em up, Cowboy Peppard and Marvelous Marty Mirrioni from the glazed donut shop. I value you all and I'm sure glad you came along when you did.

INTRODUCTION

Adolescents always generate a great deal of attention, excitement and even envy. Always in the focus of controversy and speculation, American youth first became an institution in the 50's when "pop culture" was invented by newly popularized television and the mass media. On TV sets that were rapidly saturating American homes, adults and children alike watched the "fun generation". The 50's adolescents were depicted as the group to envy—living in "suburbia" and the post-war American dream, teenagers were portrayed as a generation experiencing carefree growth and comfortable anticipation about the future.

But, unfortunately, pop portrayals and accounts of growing up are poor depictions of reality. Adolescence can be exciting but often it is not. As a prelude to adulthood, adolescence is filled with a host of questions that bear significantly on the future of a young person. Personal development is often a question of how someone fits personal style alongside the demands of society. Learning society's boundaries can be painful, expecially amidst the American perception of choice, freedom and controversy.

I became interested in the topic of youth runaways about a decade ago. This interest stemmed from the point of view that leaving home was a personal choice, sometimes constructive and somewhat difficult to accommodate. Further, I remained curious about persons who virtually abandon their home base to pursue the unknown.

Youth runaways became widespread during the late sixties, a period when movement was synonymous with growth, freedom and positive activity. However, by the early 70's, when much of the romantic mood had either shifted or died, the question became why do young people continue to leave home? Certainly much of the early motive of youth rebellion had passed, yet new reasons for leaving seemed justified.

Presently, we must understand that events in the United States have shifted toward a more reserved posture. The popular portrayal of youth on the move is no longer widely embraced or even popularly believed. Instead, youth of the 80's are immersed in an America that is slowly becoming a place that must not be taken for granted. American adolescence is still perceived as a time and place for growth, but only within quickly shrinking limitations. Increasingly, young people are coming to see that true personal exploration can only be undertaken in the face of staggering unemployment, quickly shifting technologies, and strong anxiety about the future. Unfortunately, many perspectives on youth behavior fail to acknowledge the recent developments in the United States, or their impact on earlier analysis concerning youth in America.

Much of our present analysis is unable to bridge the romantic and advocacy focused era of the 60's, with the "hip pragmatism" of the 80's. Much of the present work examines youth problems in a void that is geared toward only one timeframe.

The following book was written to bridge generational differences. The focus is on understanding the act of running away and is independent of the emotional attitudes which surround the topic. Running away may not always be a negative event and could be representative of a broader need within America. Tentatively, the mission of this book is to examine how young people construct and interpret their absences from home. It also looks at how adolescents consider the implication of their absences for family members — parents as well as siblings.

In an environment which is as quickly paced as our own, it is imperative that there is up-to-date analysis of events such as children redefining their relationships with parents. The following work was written with this thought in mind. Readers are invited to explore this analysis, not only as parents and policy makers, but also as individuals attempting to understand how others cope with and manage their worlds.

CHAPTER I

UNDERSTANDING CHILDREN AWAY FROM HOME

No, this is not my first time out of home! I have been leaving since I was thirteen. The first time caused problems. . . .cops and court. Everybody thinks being home is okay. . .I don't. . .I just can't. I don't have a home to go to. . .AND, YOU KNOW, I DON'T WANT ONE!

(Male, age fifteen)

Americans tend to take their homes for granted. From birth, the popular portrayal is that people belong someplace and have a place to go. Increasingly, this is not the case. An example is the topic of "Kids Who Run Away."

Over the last several years, "youth runaways" have received a great deal of local and national media attention. Numerous newspaper, magazine and television accounts have sketched the incidence and problematic nature of young people fleeing from their homes. Last year in the United States, approximately one million youngsters were listed as persons who had run away from their homes.[1] Of this number, a sizeable group was implicated in a range of illegal behavior by both law enforcement and youth welfare agencies. Considering the rising rate of runaways, their potential for illicit behavior and the increased press coverage of this phenomenon, it is of little surprise that both parents and law enforcement groups have become concerned about this topic. In response to growing public attention, a number of public as well as private youth advocate organizations have researched the issue. Although these investigations have provided some direction concerning the frequency and distribution of runaway behavior, they have several limitations: (1) Many rely upon inconsistent and sometimes conflicting legal definitions and stereotypes in attempting to ascertain precisely who is a runaway; (2) Often studies ignore how these stereotypes contribute to the runaway situation; (3) Little attention is devoted to the process through which the young people start to view themselves as runaways.

While present studies are of certain value, they fail to point up that "running away" is a process children engage in and not a status children arrive at. Such studies ignore the fact that few children who leave home come to immediately view themselves as runaways. Contemporary thinking has failed to demonstrate how running away differs from other sorts of youth behavior, namely the traditional delinquent. The following investigation was conducted in response to these shortcomings. Unlike earlier efforts, it does not concentrate on legal definitions or individual "disorders" to establish the identity of a runaway. Instead, it views the action of running away as a social process during which young people come to view themselves as "runaways." This process is a result of their day-to-day experiences. Similar to other forms of social behavior, becoming a runaway results from exposure to actions and attitudes of others. This exposure is instrumental in shaping the runaway role for individuals and allows them to identify with that role and ultimately be viewed as having begun a runaway career. The three concepts which are essential to this discussion are role, identity and career. Each of these concepts serve as a basis for exploring the central questions of this work: (1) Can we view running away behavior as a role, or role in process (Maines: 1983) which youth occupy as a normal course of development? (2) Can running away behavior be distinguished from the many other obvious youth behaviors now viewed as problematic (i.e., throwaways, delinquents, emancipated minors)? (3) When does somebody take on a runaway role and at what point do children disengage themselves? (Glaser and Strauss: 1971, San Giovanni: 1978, Blankenship: 1982) (4) Can we better understand the worlds of children out of their homes using their own subjective accounts?

In order to better organize this discussion, a specific

sociological framework will be relied upon and serve as an interpretive background for this effort. The framework or "theoretical prospective"[2] used here is that of "symbolic interaction". In general, this school suggests that a person's identity develops via a process of action and reaction which unfolds over time. It is an end product of an individual's utilizing action, reason and symbols (Charon, 1979:31). The culmination of this process is viewed as a "career". A career can be defined as a sequence of movements from one position to another (Becker, 1963, p. 24). The concept has been used extensively in the study of occupational systems (Hughes, 1958; Becker and Strauss, 1956) and in the investigation of deviant activities (Becker, 1963; Goffman, 1961a). A major attribute of the career model is that it accounts for a sequence of events which contribute to the shaping of one's identity. For example, in the Becker (1963) discussion of marijuana use, the focus is on each of the career steps someone goes through in order to embrace a "full-fledged" marijuana identity (p. 41). Here the development of a marijuana identity is explained by following the sequence of events which unfold through regular contact with marijuana cases. In this study, the person who comes to see him or herself as a runaway is dependent not on a pre-defined concept, but rather on experiences while away from home, on continued exposure to such experiences, and actual changes in patterns of behavior. By accounting for these day-to-day encounters, the reasons and attitudes of others, and the statements of young people themselves, it is anticipated that a clearer understanding can be achieved about how some young people come to define themselves as runaways.

The Nebulous Character of Runaway Laws

Runaway laws are somewhat nebulous and consequently no clear definition of a runaway exists — in spite of active official concern for young people who are away from their homes.

This investigation views physical absence from home as an unworkable criterion for defining an individual as a runaway. It does not distinguish a "problem" absence from a commonplace absence which is considered a normal facet of adolescent development. Furthermore, such a criterion assumes a norm among parental attitudes toward a young person's absence from the home. As a result of this ambiguity, many young persons are labeled as runaways even when their behavior does not encompass many of the recurring and common problems associated with runaway behavior.

For the most part, absence from the home is recognized under the nebulous P.I.N.S. (Persons In Need Of Supervision) statutes. Such statutes cover a variety of behaviors, including incorrigibility and absence from school, drinking, sex, disobedience, and a host of others. They tend to cover a range of offenses, and often are not clear with regard to exactly what the young person has done. There are three serious flaws in the applications of these designations:

(1) Many young people are inappropriately labeled as runaways when, in fact, either their behavior warrants other labels and reactions, or it is typical of most young persons their age. This especially occurs in jurisdictions where official court officers have few resources beyond court sanctions. The family court jurisdictions in such instances function to legitimate designations alleged by parents, school officials, etc., independent of any consistent and overt behavior (See Rubin: 1979).

Unfortunately, these reactions do little to help young people. In fact, they may be harmful. An example of this is when a young person flees home to escape physical abuse or neglect by parents. Many times the child is inappropriately charged as a runaway when in fact no such designation is justified.

(2) The existing system makes young people subject to the confused and often destructive processing of our juvenile justice system, particularly when children are placed in detention. In too many cases, official agencies use detention during the period when they are attempting to determine whether the young person needs help. While in detention, young people are often housed with idnviduals suspected of committing more serious and violent acts and often become victims of regular physical abuse.

(3) Social control agencies are often confused about who should be apprehended, thus making apprehension simply a matter of luck or timing. In a recent review of national legislation concerning runaway behavior, the United States Department of Justice reports the following con-

cerning statutory inconsistencies and problems:

> Twenty-six states within their Juvenile Codes
> make specific reference to. runaways. Arizona,
> Arkansas, Connecticut, Delaware, Indiana,
> Kentucky, Louisiana, Maine, Michigan, Mon-
> tana, Nevada, New Mexico, Oregon, Virginia,
> Ohio, Rhode Island, South Dakota and Wyo-
> ming label him a "juvenile status offender"
> (wayward, in need of supervision, unruly, etc.).
> The Wisconsin code identifies the runaway as
> being within its jurisdiction, but allows the
> judge discretion in attaching either a "delin-
> quent" or a "juvenile status offender" label.
> The California code similarly identifies the
> runaway as being within its jurisdiction, but
> does not attach a specific legal label to him.
> Finally, the New York code specifies a pro-
> cedure for the apprehension and detention of
> juveniles suspected of being runaways. This
> procedure, however, may eventually lead to the
> adjudication of the runaway as a "juvenile
> status offender." In the remaining states and
> the District of Columbia, the runaway is
> brought within the jurisdiction of the court by
> means of an "omnibus" clause. An "omnibus"
> clause is one which is broadly drafted in such a
> way as to give the court jurisdiction over al-
> most any conduct. In Colorado, Georgia,
> Idaho, Iowa, Minnesota, Missouri, New Hamp-
> shire, New Jersey, North Carolina, Texas, and
> Utah, he may be labeled a "delinquent." In
> the District of Columbia, Florida, Hawaii,
> Maryland, Massachusetts, North Dakota, Okla-
> homa, Tennessee and Vermont, he may be
> labeled a "juvenile status offender." The run-
> away in Alaska and Illinois may be labeled
> either "neglected" or a "delinquent." Finally,
> in Washington, the runaway may be labeled
> "dependent." Once adjudicated, only in Alas-
> ka, the District of Columbia, Florida, Kansas,
> Maryland, Massachusetts, North Dakota, Ohio,

5

and Tennessee, the "chronic" runaway may be institutionalized. Finally, the Interstate Compact on Juveniles provides for the out-of-state return of runaways, escapees and absconders. As of January, 1973, New Mexico was the only state that had not enacted the necessary legislation to be a member of the Compact. The return of a runaway through the Compact virtually precludes an informal disposition in that the "requisition of return" is a formal court order.[3]

Beyond the matter of legislative or jurisdictional inconsistencies, another factor which contributes to the nebulous character of running away is its "victimless" nature (Schur, 1966).

In addition, how serious running away is depends upon who the audience is. For example, for many young people, absence from home is nothing more than a ceremonial testing of strength prior to an actual departure from the nuclear family (Brennan, 1976). It is, to some, an exercise in keeping with the best traditions of America something that "naturally" occurs.

However, to many parents, law enforcement officials and youth advocates, running away represents an act which not only threatens their own basis of control but also opens a young person up to any number of abuses, dangers and problems. The immediate consequence of these dual but distinct perspectives is that no clear distinction can be made between those young persons who are engaged in "testing waters" or "seeking constructive alternatives" versus those who are "flirting with destruction" or "troubled."

Thus, in coming to define who is or is not a runaway, we are at the mercy of a host of inconsistent laws as well as a set of perceptions which do not reflect reality in either the experiences and perceptions of young people or the actual consequences of being away from home.

Running Away As A "Negative" Experience
For the most part, earlier investigations into running away behavior have viewed the issue as something negative

with runaways viewed as emotional weaklings. Moreover, when "runners" are not viewed as weaklings, they are often viewed as victims or as "different." Such perspectives foreclose on what Weber (1958) termed the "verstehen" of the situation and thus prevent us, as investigators, from "putting ourselves in another's shoes" (Jacobs, 1974, p. VIII). This approach excludes the possibility of understanding runaways in a generic sense, as contrasted with a more superficial status (i.e., away for eight hours, away the entire day, etc.). Using limited designations, we make the assumption that running away is, a priori, "bad", that people who leave home are different, inferior, etc., and that present running away definitions can legitimately do justice by distinguishing runaways from non-runaways.

Unfortunately, each of the above-mentional assumptions ignores that: (1) absence from home need not result in an official runaway designation. That is, a young person could find a legitimate role away from home and escape being labeled; (2) previously, young people were often encouraged to leave home on behalf of "seeking fortunes," but now face the regulation of social welfare, education and government groups which discourage such behavior; (3) there are distinct differences in the form and style with which parents and guardians react to absence, which in turn affects the possibility and consequences of being defined as a runaway (Brennan, 1974). Finally, (4) that in some cases the decision is the only "alternative" given the circumstances at home and parental feelings (Hackman, 1977). When looked upon together, each of these statements casts doubt on the notion that running away need always be seen as abnormal. Further, whether a youth eventually comes to be viewed as a runaway is determined less by the youth's emotional state and more by the types of reactions that occur on the part of friends, family and youth authorities.

The Development of a Runaway Role and Runaway "Career"

Since this investigation does not view the runaway role as being automatically acquired with one's leaving home, it will place a special emphasis on that process through which young people come to learn, shape and identify with and pass into the role. As suggested earlier, becoming a runaway is highly dependent on the type of encounters a young person has with family, friends and agents of social control while out of the home. For example, who is it that a young person becomes dependent upon? How do such dependencies arise and with what frequency do such dependencies continue? Are there activities which constitute a runaway role? Questions do not assume a singular understanding of running away behavior.

In tracing the development of a runaway role, it is important that a conceptual foundation be relied upon which attributes importance to the everyday events that characterize the lives of runaways. One such conceptual foundation is the notion of a "career" (Hughes, 1938; Hall, 1949; Becker, 1963; Irwin, 1970). The concept of a "career" has, as its departure point, the contact a person will have with his group. Hughes (1938) initially used the concept of a career to explore the interaction between individuals and their occupational organizations. His definition of a career defined it as something having an objective, as well as a subjective, dimension. He defined it "objectively as a series of statuses and clearly defined offices," of achievement and responsibility. Subjectively, he defined it as a moving perspective in which the person sees his life as a whole and interprets the meaning of his various attributes, actions and the things that happen to him through that total perspective (p. 409). Becker (1963) used the concept to study deviant styles among marijuana smokers, accounting for critical experiences and stages in tracing the development of such a designation. Typically, the career model points to understandings, contacts, meanings and values which are common to development in the overall career. Such a conceptual background suggests that we might look upon the emergence of a runaway role through a similar process. That is, in order for someone to be clearly considered a runaway, he must experience and pass through a set of stages typical to all persons who come to view themselves as runaways. It will be the task of this investigation to identify, where possible, particular patterns, sets of beliefs, or contingencies as they constitute a runaway role, and further, to identify how such developments contribute or modify the development of what was earlier referred to as a career.

Methodological Notes

This investigation uses a combination of interviewing, observation and analyses of available records. The overall method to be relied upon in this investigation resembles that which has been referred to by Schatzman and Strauss (1973) as "naturalist field research" (p. VI). In contrast to several earlier investigative techniques, this procedure will attempt to avoid relying on "legal" definitions and will rely as much as possible on the designations and vocabulary of the very actors who are the subject of inquiry.

The principal reason for the use of interviews, observation and records, beyond the character of the subject under study, is probably best summed up by Irwin (1970) in his own discussion of techniques used (i.e., unstructured interviews, participant accounts, group discussion and author's personal experience) in studying the careers of felons:

> This study is concerned primarily with the socially constructed perspectives, realities and moral systems of groups. These phenomena emerge and exist because persons in interaction, in order to make sense out of their surroundings and to be able to achieve their personal goals, must be able, and to some extent are able, to know what is on each other's minds. The shared perspectives, realities, and moral systems which emerge because of these two factors are best sought, therefore, by participating in the type of interaction and relying on the human capability—verstehen—which produces and sustains them. (p.5)

In summary, and taking a cue from Blumer (1969), this investigation attempts to refine the correlation between the research questions being asked and the methods used in providing answers (p. 60). It does so by locating the study within the everyday setting of our subject matter: young people who run away.

The presentation of additional chapters will conform to the following format. Chapter II will provide a survey of the literature on the topic of runaways. Chapter III is an overview and discussion of key theoretical concepts as they intersect with the interactionist perspective, the key theoretical tradition which serves as a background for this work. Chapter IV includes a discussion of methodological issues which are important to understanding how the data was collected and analyzed. In Chapter V and VI, I present findings concerning runaways. In my final chapter, I present the sociological implications and conclusions on how one becomes a runaway.

CHAPTER FOOTNOTES

[1]This estimate was reported in a testimony and conversation delivered in connection with the Runaway Youth Act of 1974, (See Title III, Juvenile Delinquency Prevention Act/ Retitled in 1980, Runaway and Homeless Youth Act).

[2]A more in-depth interpretation and discussion of this theory perspective can be found in a latter section of this book.

[3]This information is based upon review as of the end of the legislative year 1972, cited from United States Department of Justice, Law Enforcement Assistance Administration, National Criminal Justice Reference Service, Washington, D.C., August, 1978.

CHAPTER II

BACKGROUND ISSUES CONCERNING RUNAWAYS

Much contemporary thinking about "absence behavior" is seen as too preoccupied with the "treatment" and help of runaways while contradictory with respect to what treatment is supposed to accomplish. Moreover, current view and literature on the topic of child absence fails to document the central role our Family Courts play in designating a young person as a runaway. (Mann: 1980).

An explicit assumption in this investigation is that the runaway designation is a social event and result of some set of official processes (police, courts, etc.). However, much of which poses as runaway behavior are instead personal, non-problematic acts which get defined as legal public matter.

To provide a background for interpretation of the present effort, several earlier investigations and commentaries on running away will be examined here.

Historical Commentary On Children and Absence

Libertoff noted, "The runaway child was a familiar fixture in the settlement and development of the thirteen colonies" (1980:151). So the phenomenon of adolescents leaving home is one that can be traced to the early history of our nation.

But while the topic of running away has always been somewhat popular, it is only recently that law enforcement, social welfare and youth advocacy professionals have developed public policies to address this phenomenon. In fact, prior to the 60's, most of the attention on child absence had to do with the matters of child labor (Libertoff: 1980), immigrant urban poor (Bremmer: 1970), and the Family Court (Platt: 1969). Historically, children have been a source of "cheap labor" and one of America's strongest national assets. Similar to all assets, children have had to be managed both in and outside of their homes. So where children traveled to and worked and what they produced has always been a central concern for our country.

The Need For Work

Dating back to colonial days, there has always existed a need to regulate population, migration and settlement. The regulation of travel is one means of controlling the availability of a labor supply. As adults and children recognized the lack of opportunity and security in their home territories, they began to travel—seeking work opportunities (Komisar: 1977). As a result of this movement, a regular supply of labor was threatened. Lucy Komisar suggested that this development thwarted investment and speculation among entrepreneurs. In reaction to this development, speculators exercised their influence by having laws enacted against the practice of drifting or relocating. Such legislation served to make a more stable labor force possible.

Another variety of law was the anti-vagrant statutes designed to prevent drifters from becoming permanent settlers. For example, in 1655, Massachusetts passed a law giving towns the right to decide who could settle there (Komisar, 1977, p. 15). Each area was encouraged to use the British custom of "warning out" those drifters and immigrants viewed as undesirable or unfit for work (Komisar, 1977, p. 15).

In Connecticut, townspeople set a three-month limit to "warn out" anyone who became needy as a result of being sick or disabled. Similarly, Pennsylvania set up an elaborate set of statutes against non-residents, premised on the idea that such groups would simply continue to drain town revenues. The use of bonds and "head taxes" were another means of curbing the volume of migrators. The introduction and most effective use of such bonds took place in agricultural sectors, where there was a need to regulate travel and labor. In 1837, Massachusetts ordered that a bond of $1,000 be required of any persons newly arriving, who appeared to most likely become public charges (Kelso, 1972). Laws that discouraged migration became more and more prevalent as America became more commercial and centralized.

By examining reactions to people away from their regular environment, it becomes clear that a very close association was made between being away from home and being dependent on public resources. Colonial Poor Law Statutes lumped the sick, weak, disabled, newcomers, travelers, fortune seekers, vagabonds and rogues into a problem category (Komisar, 1977). Each of these groups was typically seen as tax burdens. Regular discussions in the public halls of colonial America were held on issues concerning "auctioning off the poor," "indoor versus outdoor relief,"[1] "workhouse eligibility," and the "break-up of the nuclear family" (Komisar, 1977). Regular discussion was devoted to such issues since, despite the possibility of little being accomplished, at least a forum existed for reinforcing norms regarding the regular labor supply, consistent work and production, and suspicion of the poor. A prime example of this was the public act of separating families rather than allowing them to remain together and idle.[2]

Unfortunately, most of the anti-poor statutes did much to compound the uncertainty of work and income, which further forced many into a life of constant movement in search of work. It was the poor and their children who would first experience deprivation, not being in a position to work off debts. And it was the poor who would have to flee in search of better opportunities. This condition continued into the Nineteenth Century in America. However, with the growth of cities, the concern shifted from the topic of "the poor" to the "poor in the cities."

Anthony Platt (1971) has described this as the movement toward "urban disenchantment." During the first part of the Nineteenth Century, Americans witnessed dramatic growth. The combination of technological advancement, industrialization, increased immigration from Europe, and a push to the city from surrounding areas, placed cities in desirable, popular focus. The rapid pace with which these changes and this growth occurred generated a number of concerns. These concerns focused on the urban poor. For example, overcrowded housing, ill health, broken homes, and vagabond children were all major problems associated with the city.

Overall cities were viewed from a dual perspective— while cities offered opportunities for material improvement, they also offered the opportunities for corruption, especially of children. Urban problems instigated the child-saving movement. The child-saving movement, with its middle class affiliation, was designed to improve the lives of children — especially those who were immigrants (Platt, 1969, 75). Problems among immigrant children such as poor health, little education and substandard use of language were seen as the targets of the movement. The mistreatment of children was seen as extremely prevalent and a Family Court was developed to more effectively help these children. Attending movies, fighting, expressing sexuality, staying out late at night and incorrigibility were primarily attributed to the children of the lower class. Thus, the Family Court now was in the position of dealing not only with legally defined behavior but also behavior which was distasteful (but not illegal) from a middle class perspective. This became the background for the present concern for marginal or status offenders versus actually acting-out, delinquent youth.

Despite the good intentions of the Family Court founders, today the court, in many circumstances, is not an ally to the young. How and under what circumstances a child winds up within the court's jurisdiction are usually a matter of luck and timing. This is especially true with regard to "victimless" offenses such as absence from home (Schur, 1965; Platt, 1972). Such offenders often find their way to court either through the plea of a desperate parent or via arrest in a totally unrelated matter.

There is a growing body of literature which tends to support the idea that public intervention by authorities on behalf of youth can hurt more than help (Elliott and Aceton: 1979).

The Creation Of A Juvenile Court

In order to encourage the notion of treatment rather than punishment, a whole new vocabulary was created along with the Juvenile Court. Juvenile Courts employ petitions instead of complaints, initial hearings instead of arraignment, and disposition rather than sentence. The courts were to be informal and protectors of juveniles well-being. Lawyers, transcripts and other trappings of adult court were thought to be harmful. The court process was not to be an adversary proceeding as in adult criminal courts.

14

Structurally, the Juvenile Court provides separate courtrooms, separate records and informal procedures. According to the act, the "care, custody and discipline of a child shall approximate as nearly as may be that which should be given by its parents. . . ." (Smith and Pollack, 1973).

The establishment of a court was to bring a further dimension which remains a central quality of the Family Court; namely, control over marginal behavior. Platt (1972) reports that the court's creation brought within governmental control "a set of youthful activities that had been previously ignored or handled informally" (p. 139). The behavior selected to be penalized by the child savers—drinking, begging, roaming the streets, frequenting dance halls, themselves family problems which ultimately grew more problematic.

The young person who depends on the court for "official" direction eventually comes to view himself (or is viewed) as different or deviant. Thus, the Family Court is an irony because while attempting to help or assist children, it can exacerbate their problems.

Family Court Routine

Family Court's jurisdiction encompasses PINS (Persons in Need of Supervision), neglected children and juvenile delinquents. For people in New York State, Family Court involvement is initiated at the Probation Intake Unit, an auxiliary arm of the court. As is typical in most states, the Family Court is a court of limited jurisdiction and its power is limited to the specialized types of issues (i.e., domestic) assigned to its jurisdiction.

To initiate a DC (Delinquent Charge) Petition or PINS Petition, the potential petitioner(s) (parents, police, school, citizens) must bring the matter to the Probation Intake Unit of Family Court, where the Intake Probation Officer (IPC) meets with the involved parties. In many instances, the type of petition which is drawn up may depend on extraneous factors such as the identity of the respondent, his language and demeanor, rather than on the nature of the respondent's actual behavior. Many of the cases which reach the court are PINS cases since the PINS statute is vague and is often used as a catch-all category for bringing cases to court.

The wording of the PINS statute contained in the Family Court Act is very loose and subject to many interpretations. As a result, almost any child can be brought to court under its provisions and detentioned under its provisions. Furthermore, there are no uniform, generally accepted criteria for determining precisely what type of behavior constitutes being "incorrigible," "ungovernable," "habitually away," "disobedient," and "beyond the lawful control of parent or other lawful authority." Police, judges and other court officials are given a great deal of discretion in evaluating the juvenile's behavior and making decisions. This often leads to abuses of authority — often a juvenile is not judged on behavior but on certain characteristics such as race, age, socio-economic status, appearance, etc., which have little or no bearing on his actions. In the case of runaways, this is especially true, since they often make a poor impression on the court (usually having little means of support or protection and often exhibiting a general mistrust of court personnel).

In some Family Court cases, a petition need not be drawn at all. Instead of drawing a petition, an officer can either adjourn or adjust a case informally. When dealing with runaways, this is synonymous with "doing nothing" for the child. This practice is often justified on the grounds that it diverts children from a formal process and thus prevents children from being stigmatized by a court record. It also assumes that some kind of action is taken to prevent a child from continuing his or her runaway behavior.

To compound this problem, informal processing is of limited usefulness in runaway cases since the Intake Unit mentioned above does not have the power to prevent a court hearing if the parent desires it. Further, it cannot compel the juvenile to appear at any conference, produce papers, or visit any places; i.e., social agency, employment office; and there can be no adjustment if the juvenile denies running away. Yet young people who are before the court as alleged "undomiciled," "incorrigible," or "ungovernable," understand the significance of what is taking place. They are being brought to court for behavior which is not only nebulous with regard to its consequences, but is also sporadic in occurrence. Many young people recognize that the court is being used to cope with the interest and confusion of the parents or guardians and does little to deal with underlying problems.

There appears to be at least three reasons for why the court has failed to deal with specific youth issues such as absence. First, from its inception, the court has addressed too wide a range of behavior to be effective. In many cases, the Family Court has not been able to alter a child's behavior or the behavior of the child's family via coercion. The mandate of the Family Court regarding incorrigible or wayward children remains too broad and too dependent on family cooperation. Second, in the past decade, many Family Courts have simply given their runaway statutory responsibilities over to social services agencies. Often such transfer of authority is undertaken after the court has proven non-responsive. Such actions make the court look indecisive. Third, much of the theoretical explanation about runaway and youth absence has been inconclusive and shifting. Consequently, courts have shifted postures regarding how and what should be done with runaways. For example, courts that embrace runaway prevention programs (an outgrowth of non-intervention — to be discussed) in some cases are punitive in dealing with some children in other cases.

A central position of this study is that most, if not all, thinking about runaway behavior is too preoccupied with viewing the person as a "victim," "culprit" or "problem." Involvement in the Family Court casts an immediate image which depicts the person's experiences, lifestyle, etc., as negative or bad and as something which cannot be directed towards a conventional lifestyle. A major consequence of court involvement is that only negative aspects of the runaway style are examined while ignoring the issues of 1) when someone is an actual runaway versus a person flirting with the idea of exploring alternative lifestyles, etc.; 2) identifying major tuning points in the absence process; 3) understanding how social situations contribute to changes in perceptions about absence.

Psychopathological Understanding of Runaways

Much thinking within the Family Court is based upon

the concept that individuals experiencing problems can be helped or reformed. Rehabilitative and reformist thinking have occupied significant roles in thinking about runaways. Several distinct schools have emerged in attempting to explain the problematic nature of absence behavior. While each school attempts to focus on the individual, each school is distinct in its explanatory scheme and research.

One of the most popular schools of thought about the understanding of runaways is the psychopathological. This school is also the oldest and probably the most instrumental in providing a guide on underlying ideology to child savers, the Family Court and people changing groups. The psychopathological school links runaway behavior to individual defects and developmental problems. For example, Armstrong (1938), as a result of studying youth before the New York County Family Court, concluded that: a) Runaways tended to have abnormal or sub-intelligence; and b) Obvious mental defects. Rumer (1940), a psychiatrist at Brooklyn State Hospital, concluded that those youth identified as runaways could be described as youth who were "overly deficient, assaultive, disruptive and deficient when contrasted with other types of youth."

Frederick Rosenheim (1940) changed directions in the line of inquiry when he suggested that, based upon his extensive examination of case histories of youths undergoing treatment, males running away often did so as a result of a continued inability to resolve Oedipus impulses. The inability to do so brings on guilt and triggers the runaway episode.

In a much later investigation of Massachusetts court cases, Robby, et al (1964) found that young women respondents fleed their homes because of the threat of an incestuous relationship with the father. Several authors have tried to develop typologies of runaways based upon their emotional makeup and their likes and dislikes. Although these efforts have provided a very thin line between an individual versus a collective understanding, several tend to stress a person pathology. McReady (1971) identified two major types of young people in her caseload: A group which was devoted to the "seeking of pleasure" and who devoted their energies to that pursuit, and a second group which was in search of work and ran away to find an opportunity to work.

Richard Jenkins (1971), upon examination of a cross-section of runaways, characterized some youth as having a "runaway reaction." Young people exhibiting this "runaway reactive" behavior were reported as typically running away to escape a threat situation. Typically, they were immature and timid youth who report rejection from home, few friends and feelings of inadequacy. However, several studies refute the claims made regarding the pathological nature of runaway behavior. For example, Kaufman and Allen (1965) point out that running away may be only one phase of a young person's life which at that time is filled with problems that will eventually be overcome. In their Haight-Ashbury investigation, they point to resourcefulness and problem-solving skills of such runaways.

Comparing a group of so-called runaways with a similar control, they found little difference between the way either group approached a wide range of adolescent obstacles. Considering this finding from a psychological viewpoint, investigations disagree about abilities of runaways.

The Reformists

A second group of runaway investigators are called reformists. The reformists use a synthesis of a psychopathological stance and a milieu therapeutic approach to runaways. Investigations in this category typically try to locate causes of chronic absence behavior in the home or other environmental setting of subjects, so such behavior can be modified. The assumption here is that if there is appropriate rehabilitation or assistance provided to the problematic setting (i.e., home, school, etc.), the individuals will not feel the strain which propels them into the runaway scene.

This group is comparable to the adult rehabilitation movement in the adult criminal justice circles. Their acceptance of a positivist criminology, coupled with a reformist ideology, has served as the basis for undertaking regular rehabilitative attempts. However, in recent years, criminal rehabilitation has been severely criticized in particular by authorities who feel they simply cannot do so or afford to do so and even prisoners who feel victimized in the name of treatment. (Schur: 1974, Von Hirsch: 1977) Unlike those taking the psychopathological position, the reformists do not locate all causes of runaway behavior in the makeup of the individual.

What is stressed by reformist is the predisposition or situation (Roberts: 1981) which under the right degree of strain, can cause acting out, or incorrigible runaway behavior. The reformist position uses both personality and environment to explain runaway behavior. For example, Foster (1966) pointed out that: "A separation between parent and child ultimately leads to runaway behavior since it serves to intensify a child's fear of rejection and thus makes it difficult to cope with any felt anger or frustration." Another example is found in Stierlin (1973), who classified four types of runaways based upon a number of family dynamics which a young person either engages in or fails to engage in. Depending upon the degree of family involvement, runaways were typed as abortive, lonely schizoid, crisis prone or casual runaways. In certain cases, an emphasis is shifted to being more individual or more environmental as in the case of the Hildebrand (1963) investigation of runaway youth in the Brooklyn section of New York. Hildebrand (1963), found that the "most influential factor that could explain the continued and prolonged absence from home was deprivation." Almost all of the respondent group reported or identified severe problems with education, school or health. Ambrisino (1972) identified similar patterns and, like Hildebrand (1963), suggested that those youth identified as "chronic runaways" normally come from family backgrounds exhibiting severe deprivation.

Considering the identification of deprivations, a significant emphasis in the reformist approach is to develop help strategies that will aid certain youth and their families Libertoff (1976), for example, undertook an investigation on how certain types of family program interventions can improve the family problems of runaways. He identified two program types, one being Parent Effectiveness Training (PET) in which parents are trained to better manage their children and themselves. The second is a public education program for parents directed at making them more familiar with early warning signs of troubled behavior identified among runaways. Items such as fighting, temper tantrums, truancy and solitary behavior are all viewed as early signs of a runaway behavior. In an earlier effort, Libertoff (1974) analyzed interviews conducted among 85 young people and their families to understand the extent programs have impacted on the lives of runaways. The study focused on the program's ability to produce any reform in the runaway's family setting. Libertoff's (1974) report is, for the most part, favorable towards programs since the majority of his response group "found the program helpful, would contact the programs again if necessary and would recommend the projects to friends" (p. 23).

Contrasting a reformist perspective with a psychopathological perspective, it is appropriate to suggest that the former has proved more productive than the latter. For example, as an offshoot of the Libertoff investigation mentioned above, authorities have come to believe that "much of what we know about runaway children is a direct reflection of the type of agency that has controlled, treated and/or served young people" (Libertoff, 1974). This statement is important when evaluating the quality of information we have about runaways. It prompts us into asking such questions as: "Who is it that we have chosen to study?" "Is this person somehow different because of the predicament we find him in, rather than because of an emotional predisposition?" Such questions have served a critical role in reevaluating the psychopathological basis for running away, and they seem to be a result of reformist investigative energies.

Another example is found in the identification of 65 information networks used by youths away from home. Over time, reformists have identified a police-legal network, a mental health, social welfare, youth advocate, and an adult-peer network. Of more significance is the discovery that some youth rely on little or no network contact, and that very little is known about them. Such detail is important when going beyond individual explanations, even though this might not have been the original intention of the reformists.

Delinquency Focused Research

A third perspective exists concerning runaways, and I have labeled this "delinquency-focused research." The typical concern here is estimating or determining the distribution of delinquency among runaways. Questions are asked such as: How much delinquent behavior can be attributed to runaways, or how many runaways have had previous contact with the law?

A recent example of this is an investigation (Brennan, 1976) concerning the diversity of runaway populations and the respective incidence of runaway behavior reported within each. Brennan's (1976) conclusion is that, "In general, runaways are indeed more delinquent than non-runaways." This finding is based upon a national probability sample of youth ranging in age from ten through sixteen, who resided in various regions throughout the United States. Brennan's effort was an outgrowth of two earlier efforts which generally identified types and incidences of delinquent and incorrigible behavior, and tested the "National Theory of Youth Delinquency" (Dunform, 1975; Brennan, Brewington and Walker, 1974). These investigations reported distinct types of runaways (i.e., fortune seekers versus confused youth, etc.) and compared rates of delinquent behavior. Also, a good deal of variability existed between actual levels of reported delinquency and specific runaway types.

Banouhl and Van Houten (1976) have criticized the Brennan investigation (1976) for arriving at such conclusions. It is their position that the Brennan sampling and analytic procedures were biased toward the inclusion of too many delinquent-prone youth. An over-reporting of delinquent behavior is the result.

However, Martin Gold of the Institute of Group Dynamics for Social Research, University of Michigan, supports the conclusions cited by Brennan with his own data, which was gathered in the Institute's National Survey of Youth for 1967 and 1962. Though the conclusions were the same as those reached by Brennan, the analytic procedures were somewhat different. These conclusions were presented before the **Subcommittee on Equal Opportunities on Juvenile Justice and Delinquency Prevention and Runaway Youth**.[3]

In some cases, the data-gathering effort within delinquency-focused groups is done within delinquency contexts or in connection with a self-help effort, such as a runaway program. One such study, conducted by Glick and Robinson (1976), estimated the actual numbers of runaways living in New York City, their delinquent activity, and their service

22

needs. Respondents were gathered from temporary shelter locations set up by the research groups. The effort was entitled, *Emergency and Youth on the Run Project*. This type of investigation is important in understanding the sorts of needs, problems, etc., young people have while away from home. This dimension is extremely critical to youth service decision-makers. However, just how much understanding such investigations contribute to how one becomes or believes one's self to be a runaway is somewhat open for discussion. Such efforts ignore certain generic features of a runaway research context which foreclose on important pieces of data. In particular, the application of specific survey designs which rely upon standard items, standard language and meaning, as well as "one shot data collection" are all limited methodologically and, therefore, make it most difficult to account for the social basis of human conduct or the fluidity characteristic of a runaway setting. Furthermore, such design suggests that many of the daily events which are part of the scene are already understood by all participants. This tends to close out important insights concerning the entire process of running away. However, such a criticism can be leveled at research methods other than survey design and is not only a problem of this technique.

A second problem is the assumption that once someone leaves home, he or she is, for all intents and purposes, a runaway, and can be researched as such! Such a position ignores the fact that there is a cumulative process which should be looked at when deciding who is a runaway and that many young people understand what is expected of them as runaways, know the ropes and have no ambivalence toward the designation. Ignoring such concerns, these studies do little to point out how and at what point the individual away from home begins to view him or herself as a runaway.

Legal Non-Intervention Thinking

A fourth group is the legalist-non-interventionist-thinkers. The legalist-non-interventionist is in marked contrast to each of the three previously mentioned perspectives, (Schur, 1974). The central position in this line of thought is that, "given the rather questionable and often harmful influence of the juvenile court and 'juvenile justice system'," it makes sense to "leave children alone as much as possible rather than involve them in court." That is, non-intervention is better than harmful intervention. In his book entitled, *Radical Non-Intervention*, Edwin Schur (1974) explores some of the earlier concepts concerning the definition of delinquent. He also paints a picture of how our official images of delinquency (in theory) shape the public reaction toward delinquency.

For example, if we view misbehavior among children as a product of some character defect, then our reaction toward delinquent behavior will focus on removing the defect instead of some other strategy. Such a strategy assumes the ability to detect, diagnose and treat such defects in exact terms—skills which to date remain inconsistent (Irwin, 1970; Frankel, 1972; Von Hirsh, 1977). Thus, the position taken by the non-interventionist is that the state, while intervening for its own good reasons, is doing little to help many children.

Several other authors have indirectly supported this notion. For example, David Matza (1970) has questioned the foundation upon which just outcomes are reached in the juvenile court; that is, what fair standards might be used to understand when justice has been achieved—from the perspective of the child observing the proceedings. Sanford Katz has questioned our Nineteenth Century court procedure of protecting children, especially because of the new standards and issues surrounding children in the Twentieth Century.

Today, the characteristic style of life found in the United States often places the court in a moral entrepreneur role. Parents often expect the court to referee or coerce young people to pursue an "acceptable lifestyle" in the midst of quickly changing norms and values both inside and outside the court. However, the Family Court itself has undergone significant structural changes. Consequently, it may not be able to assist parents.

Several authors have commented recently that more change has occurred inside the Family Court than was being experienced outside in society at large. Decisions such as that of Gault and Ellery C. altered the daily activities of the court in dealing with children. No longer are procedural and due process issues dismissed in the name of treatment. Children are now assumed to be entitled to many of the Constitutional Due Process Safeguards provided to adults being processed in Criminal Courts. (See President's Task Force on Juvenile Justice) In many cases, children suffer through the stigma and strain of continued court contact without obtaining an acceptable resolution for the child or the parent.

The non-interventionists question whether a Family Court can assist young people or contribute any sort of resolution to their problems. This point most clearly separates this perspective from the others since it appears to focus on (1) the organization rather than the individual in examining deviant behavior, (2) the organization as a possible producer of combined deviance, and (3) the perspective that use of Family Court as a manager of conflict is inappropriate, or at least incomplete.

Given the push toward procedural safeguards in Family Court proceedings, it appears that this situation is not likely to improve, but rather worsen. Due process implies the need for "systematic outlines" in establishing facts, and also a "combative" model of justice using a defense and prosecution. Unfortunately, such a development may pinpoint legal guilt, but it does not pinpoint youth problems. It has been suggested elsewhere that such a condition represents an incomplete structure, since it requires great amounts of time and an adherence to rules of procedure. However, parties in Family Court proceedings often have no clear understanding of what the family is, or what can be done. Such parties often have an ambivalent feeling toward the court and seek a referee and confidante, rather than a seeker of innocence of guilt.

The foundation upon which the non-interventionist perspective rests is that of a labeling perspective (Lemert, 1951; Becker, 1961; Schur, 1974). The labeling perspective which is most closely allied with a sociological perspective, traditionally placed a good deal of emphasis on actor "interaction" in the establishment of meaning. In this perspective, individual actors within a court setting become labeled through a reciprocal process of action and reaction (Schur:1974)

Becoming a runaway is not dependent upon personal motivation but rather upon daily interaction which clarifies, modifies, and confirms such a role. For example, juvenile laws, Family Court and youth detention facilities are all capable of applying the runaway label to young persons away from home, and often do so. The fact that this occurs and that young people are processed as such is seen here as something that contributes to young persons becoming viewed as runaways and later coming to view *themselves* in that status. This interaction between the child as actor and agents of control (i.e., police, courts, etc.) is the primary concern of interactionists and legalists alike.

In summary, when considering our understandings about "runaways," several problems become apparent. First: Many of the studies on runaway behavior assume individual differences, without an appreciation for the role official agents play in creating such differences. Many children who encounter help agents and agencies are simply not helped. The Family Court is a case in point (some children leave with more problems). Second: Few empirical studies exist which demonstrate the presence of runaway behavior over a long period of time. Little longitudinal data exists on the runaway child, and even less information about actual events in the absence network. Third: While significant attention has been focused on absence from home, much of this has been of a dramatic nature. Examining events from a dramatic viewpoint often serves to confuse the issue of which children are in need of help. Not all children who leave home need or want help. Moreover, to date, many of the young people who leave home often do so for their own protection. It is difficult, given the emotional nature of the runaway topic, to either plan or anticipate what is an appropriate youth service. Fourth: Writers on the subject of runaways have yet to fully depict the dismal failure of the Family Court in addressing this issue. Family Courts are simply not equipped to meet the needs of either child or family. Fifth: Most of these studies measure or identify some individual problems runaways possess. The implicit assumption being all children don't experience such events as part of growing up. Sixth: Most of these studies provide little information about other significant persons who confirm the runaway identity. Certainly children depend on persons other than their parents once they leave home. It still remains unclear who these people are. Seventh: Many studies ignore or confuse the distinction between young people seeing themselves as runaways versus official agents or parents designating children as delinquents. Finally, in many runaway studies, no indication is given as to when children disengage themselves from a role like that of a runaway. For example, isn't it possible for children to have "temporary excursions" into the lifestyle of being a runaway as a form of experimentation? No one is totally immersed in one specific role all of the time. From a sociological point of view, this is an important issue because running away could be conceived not as a final product but a "product in process." (Maines: 1983) That is, children become runaways based upon what is made of this act socially! Much like other social designations, the "runaway" is a variable status that actors pass in and out of.

CHAPTER FOOTNOTES

[1]The difference between both is that "indoor relief" required residence in a poor house, whereas "outdoor relief" was rendered in the immediate community.

[2]Little recognition was then made about the potential harm that a policy could generate, especially with respect to utilizing the nuclear family as a means of social control.

[3]A complete discussion of this matter can be found in *Youth Alternatives*, May, 1976, Washington, D.C.

CHAPTER III

THEORETICAL ASSUMPTIONS AND FOUNDATIONS

Within this investigation, the concept of children "running away" or being defined runaway is viewed as problematic. The runaway designation is viewed as problematic for three reasons. First, being a runaway is viewed as a role behavior. Like other societal roles and behaviors, running away must be learned through a process of conscious activity. Running away is not an automatic status. Second, unlike other roles readily identifiable within a social structure (i.e., mother, father), running away has no clearcut role attributes. No clear "script" exists as to what children must do to be viewed as having run away. For example, some parents, upon the discovery of absences by their child, view them as runaways. In contrast, Hackman (1978) reports the reality of some parents asking their children to leave. That is, parents and children coming to a mutual agreement that the home is no longer a reasonable place for the child to remain in. Third, this effort does not view being a runaway as a static event, but rather as a status which is in the state of flux. Because no set role behavior exists, actors are constantly attempting to define, refine and fit themselves alongside others they encounter in the world away from home. As noted by Glaser and Strauss (1971:47), "persons are in constant movement over time, not just in a status." Becoming a runaway is viewed here as a process. A process of identifying learning, believing and in some cases abandoning activities which are encountered in the out of home experience.

In order to structure the present investigation, some reference to a theory viewpoint will be made. In relying on such a viewpoint, the concepts of meaning, identity and "committing" (Becker: 1961) oneself to the runaway role can be more easily understood. The role of theory will be used here to "inform" rather than to test suppositions about the world (Smylka:1981). Theory serves here as an informing background and as something which lends insight, concept and perspective when viewing runaways. As used here, theory provides a general orientation from which research efforts proceed. The use of theory is a reference point for the empirical problem of when is somebody a runaway.

The primary object is to understand the everyday lives of children living away from home and to delineate the social implications of their everyday behavior. As a sociologist studying children, I have attempted to link individual acts to the social worlds in which they unfold, and to appreciate how actors construct their worlds and live within them. As Douglas has pointed out about the task of the sociologist:

> A basic question for all sociologists becomes that of how these social meanings are to be determined: how are we to truthfully and reliably get at this fundamental data of all our sociological research and theory? The only truthful answer is that in some way we must rely upon our understandings of everyday life, gained through direct observations of that life and always involving the use of our own commonsense understandings derived from our direct involvements in it.
>
> (Douglas: 1970)

In general terms, the theoretical perspective to be relied upon in the research can best be termed an "interactionist" perspective. In using this term, the investigator will try to convey a set of aspects and demands similar to those expressed by Jacobs (1973, p. v) in his own description of an interactionist perspective. . .

> By an interactionist perspective I mean. . .those aspects which concern themselves with such subjective social-psychological considerations as the individual's intentions, motives and morals as these relate to the more general sociological problem of establishing the reality of this social science. This (perspective) re-

quires that the researcher achieve an understanding of the social meaning of social actions, as these are perceived by members of the social settings. The interactionist perspective contends that meaning of verbal and nonverbal communications do not inhere in the words or deeds themselves but are conferred upon one's works and deeds by others.

Another term often used to describe this perspective is the "interpretive paradigm" of social interaction (Wilson, 1970; Drietzel, 1971; Hawkins and Tideman, 1975). Hawkins and Tideman (1975, p. 6) have traced this perspective mainly to the work of symbolic interactionists like Turner (1962), who view interaction as a "role-making and remaking" from within the interaction sequence. Such a position makes particular assertions about social interaction which, when summarized, take the following form: first, the actor is assumed to place the behavior of others into patterns or roles (Hawkins and Tideman, 1975, p. 6). Second, such an assignment process is based on some imputation of motives to "actors by others" (Zimmerman, 1970, p. 12). Third, the interaction sequence is characterized by a certain level of uncertainty, of an assignment and reassignment of roles (Hawkins and Tideman, 1975, p. 7).

When looking at an overview of the interactionist interpretive position, it can by no means be seen as a unified perspective. For example, Maines (1978, p. 49) points out that there are several ways in which a statement on interaction can be written; that is, it can take the point of view of society, the self, or the interaction. These distinct perspectives have announced themselves in a host of investigations, each representing distinct viewpoints. However, despite this diversity, this perspective can provide a wide breadth of influence to the present investigation, especially as it applies to concern for actor "meaning." Meaning, for all intents and purposes, is the most unifying theme for interactionist thought. Hurbert Blumer (1969), a central figure in interactionist thinking, makes this clear when he suggests that:

The first premise is that human beings act toward things on the basis of the meanings that

the things have for them. . . The second premise is that the meaning of such things is de-
rived from, or arises out of, the social interaction that one has with one's fellows. The
third premise is that these meanings are handled in, and modified through, an interpretive
process used by the person in dealing with the
things he encounters. (p. 2)

In all three premises, the matter of meaning is of central importance. Each premise dwells on the issues of seeking,
developing and establishing meaning, with nothing taken for
granted. This investigator believes that Blumer (1969) in his
presentation of these promises goes "beyond providing basic
information" about theory, to include the perspective that
actors' meanings are usually ignored or taken for granted in
social science discussion. He notes,

Meaning is either taken for granted and
thus pushed aside as unimportant or it is regarded as a more neutral link between the
factors responsible for human behavior and
this behavior as the product of such factors. We
can see this clearly in the predominant posture
of psychological and social science today. Common to both of these fields is the tendency to
treat human behavior as the product of various
factors that play upon human beings, therefore, concern is with the behavior and with the
factors regarded as producing them. Thus,
psychologists turn to such factors as stimuli,
attitudes, conscious or unconscious motives,
various kinds of psychological inputs, perception and cognition, and various features of
person organization to account for given
forms or instances of human conduct. In a
similar fashion, sociologists rely on such factors as social position, status demands, social
roles, cultural prescriptions, norms and values,
social pressures and group affiliation to provide
such explanations. In both such typical psychological and sociological explanations, the

31

meanings of things for the human beings who
are acting are either bypassed or swallowed up
in the factors used to account for their behavior. (p. 2)

For Blumer, the alternative must be to seek meaning as a
product and as something to be explained rather than as
something accidental to action.

If the three above premises are translated into one
entire act, the significance of each should at once become
clear for the production of meaning. In premise one, the
actor is, through his own reflective processes, "picking out
events" which confront him. The actor can, in this instance,
be seen as providing self indications to himself about events.
In premise two, we approach the issue of meaning, by virtue
of having other actors who confirm our "hunches" about the
meanings things have for us. At this level, actors can provide
confirmation for us about meaning by the way they act
(i.e., agreement, as expected, etc.). Finally, in premise three,
we "create," from our own input and from the input of
others, a final version of meaning based upon whatever our
original perception of meaning was. This final premise implies a self-confirmation process, a "once-and-for-all" method
of establishing meaning. Blumer (1963) has referred to this as
"the actor making indications to himself" (p. 3). Upon reaching this point, the actor can proceed into his next phase of
activity, having used a meaning as a basis on which to respond.

For interactionists, the significance of meaning is that
it guides action—that is, through a process of "producing
meanings," we can realize a set of action sequences for the
self. Once made, concrete meanings help guide what we are
"supposed to do."

George Herbert Mead (1934) elaborated on this process and suggested that action becomes possible through
"communication between our self's as objects," and others
Mead noted:

The individual experiences himself as such,
not directly, but only indirectly, from the
particular standpoints of other individual members of the same social group, or from the

32

generalized standpoint of the group as a
whole to which he belongs. For he enters
his own experience as a self or individual, not
directly or immediately, not by becoming a
subject to himself, but only insofar as he first
becomes an object to himself just as other individuals are objects to him or in his experience; and he becomes an object to himself
only by taking the attitudes of other individuals toward himself within a social environment or context of experience and behavior
in which both he and they are involved. The
importance of what we term 'communication'
lies in the fact that it provides a form of behavior in which the organism or the individual may become an object to himself.

Thus, by "taking the role" of other actors ("others"
in Mead's terms), action on behalf of communication becomes possible. That is, action becomes predicated on
being able to anticipate others' responses by virtue of looking at the role of the other. This is the essence of communication. Communication among actors may be seen as a
process of reflecting upon the actions of others, or, to put
it in another way, "to find out what each of us means to
the other." However, if we look at the above quote, we at
once recognize his reference to a "self as object" on behalf
of realizing this communication process.

The Manufacturing of a Runaway Role

The concept of role is basic to all consistent human
action and reaction. Roles provide personal scripts for individuals within the many world situations they find themselves in. Roles ultimately link individuals to their group,
and ultimately enable the person to clarify what is happening
or what is supposed to happen. As Lee has suggested:

Societal roles are prescribed by the conventions and morals of a society. Just as societal institutions represent configurations of
conventions and morals in terms of broadly
felt needs, interests, and wishes, so societal

roles are configurations of conventions and morals in terms of the man-as-he-should-be in some area of social life.

(Lee, 1969:18)

As the concept of a role applies to runaways, the concern here is how does the individual come to recognize, learn, refine and embrace the acts which comprise a runaway role. Furthermore, how is the runaway role contructed from that "loose"set of activities children engage in once out of the home. This investigation views the runaway role as something that is "socially manufactured" by the individual. Once out of the home, runaway roles become created by children. Rather than stepping into a set of expectations understood to be the behavior of runaways, children are interpreting who they are. The role of runaway provides a base for the child interpretation and in recognizing and declaring "I am a runaway" or conversely, "I am not a runaway." In the present investigation, the role of runaway must be seen as constructed in an interaction setting. Children become runaways only after they come to recognize, learn and identify events important to persons living out of their homes. Consequently, the concept of role is always dependent on what we as individuals interpret about the persons and symbols around us. Children out of their homes can only locate themselves and believe themselves to be runaways after being located by others. Thus the runaway role is dependent for its "construction" not on the person alone but also by the numerous groups and organization encounters that make up the person's day. To paraphrase the vocabulary of George Herbert Mead, the runaway individual is constantly rectifying the differences that exist between their "I" (a person's subjective essence or self) and their "me" (a person's standard or reference for what behavior ought to be). Unless the child can establish a perfect fit between the "who I am" (Mead's notion of self) and "who I ought to be" (Mead's notion of a standard for self to ponder about), the person will never be immersed within a runaway role. The child may become immersed in a delinquent, young adult or "word of the court" role, but not that of runaway. To become a runaway is to establish your identity as runaway and to have that identity established by others. And it is the concept of identity that is now considered.

Concern for Identity

A third major preoccupation among interactionists has to do with the identity of individuals and how such identity emerges from within one's encounters with others. Further, how such an identity (i.e., runaway) is confirmed.

As viewed here, this is a problem of recognizing someone's assumed versus their confirmed identity. McCall and Simmons (1975) view this as a process of "protecting of the self." Protecting one's identity is important for two reasons. First, individual actors, upon arriving at a new situation, require some sense of involvement in order to be part of the situation (i.e., children out of their homes). Thus, actors must busy themselves in arriving at a definition of the situation via the clues each participant gives off about themselves. Goffman (1959) depicts this concern when he explored the "dramaturgical perspective" in his work, *The Presentation of Self in Everyday Life*, (p. 105). He writes:

> When an individual enters the presence of others, they commonly seek to acquire information about him or bring into play information about him already possessed. . . However, during the period in which the individual is in the immediate presence of others, few events may occur which directly provide the others with the conclusive information they need if they are to direct wisely their own activity (p. 4)

Implicit in this passage is the idea that within every social interaction, there is a good deal of distance between what a specific situation will tell others about an individual versus what he truly is.

Within sociology, the concern for identity normally extends beyond the question of how identity is established to include transformation in social interaction For our purposes how children move from being absentees, delinquents, victims of adventure seeks to full-fledged runaways.

Matters such as "cycles," "turning points," and "careers," are referred to in explaining how identities become known to actors, how they become routinized, and how they change.[1] For the most part, identities once achieved through interaction are not "once and for all" end products. Strauss (1969), for example, in his discussion on the act of naming suggests that actors constantly are achieving transformation by virtue of how differently they identify:

> The renaming of any object, then, amounts to a reassement of your relation to it and *ipso facto* your behavior becomes changed along the line of your reassessment. In any event, it is the definition of what it "is" that allows action to occur with reference to what it is taken to be. (p. 22)

A similar concern seems implied by Becker in how alternatives occur in a person's assessment of marijuana use. Initially someone may not see themselves as a "user;" however, after reaching certain milestones common to and recognized by users, a transformation is possible and a new identity can emerge.

New situations present new threats. Actors are trying to locate themselves, trying to establish their self vis-a-vis other self's. Given the possibility that not all actors will present a total self, an individual self, the issue becomes one of protection. Two, most social action takes place with a kind of beforehand understanding of what it is that will or should take place. Strauss (1969) suggests that this is done through a process of naming and classifying (p. 15). Thus, it is important that we, as social creatures, understand that regardless of what we may feel part of, how we will be identified is dependent upon how we are seen. One's true identity may never be revealed so long as one manages to present the facade that some other actor anticipates. As Strauss (1969) notes:

> . . .identity is connected with the fateful appraisals made of oneself—by one self and by others. Everyone presents himself to others and to himself, and sees himself in the mirrors of their judgments. The masks he then and thereafter presents to the world and its citizens

are fashioned upon his anticipation of their judgments. (p. 9)

What the implication of this social presentation holds for our personal identity is that we can hold on to it without drawing from a collective setting. We can, to an extent, be seen as having a repertoire of identities, each more public or overt than the next, each more or less important depending upon the situation in question. McCall and Simmons (1966) have viewed this in terms of "hierarchiers" (p. 218) and of selective actor perception (p. 95). They note:

> . . .we find, first of all, that people employ a good deal of selective perception of their own actions. The individual knows in a general, though not necessarily consciously thought out, sense that identities he is laying claim to and attempting to fulfill through his actions, and he can, therefore, ignore and disattend those features of his conduct that are not relevant parts of the performance of these roles. Unfortunately, the person's other audiences typically lack this knowledge and consequently they can never be sure what is message and what is noise. (p. 95)

Beyond keeping one's identities separate or covert, the individual act can also rely on other means for protecting self. For example, McCall and Simmons (1966) refer to the processes of "rationalization" (explaining away the episode) and "scapegoating" (blaming someone else) as methods for handling social discrepancies, should they arise. Indeed, such discrepancies often have the potential for arising in social settings and it is to the benefit of each individual actor that identities not be spoiled since we run the risk of interrupting lines of action or of having to manage the spoiled identity (Goffman, 1967). Such outcomes are not desired or idealized choices in consistent social encounters, yet they sometimes become necessary, giving the unfolding of certain events or embarrassments which periodically occur.

Commitment and Career

The final issues of relevance have to do with the matters of career and commitment. In contrast to the earlier matters, the concern here is not for how meaning gets collectively established, but rather how it is sustained. Further, can a reasonable framework be referred to which allows us to monitor such a sustained collective activity? The concept of commitment (Becker, 1960; Stebbins, 1973) allows us to address the first issue, that of sustained behavior; the use of "career," the second (Becker, 1961 and Hughes, 1958; Goffman, 1961; Glaser, 1963).

In using the concept of commitment, Becker (1961) is concerned with how collective activity gets sustained through a process of interaction. He suggests that such commitments are particular consequences or constraints which contribute to the routine and consistent action conduct. Becker (1961) rejects earlier explanations of commitment, which he refers to as tautological.

Instead, Becker seeks to understand the process of "being committed" beyond the immediate activity which the concept is designed to explain. He does this by use of his concept of "side bets." A side bet is a previously made agreement, understanding or investment, etc., which functions to structure off alternative lines of action, and tends to lock an actor into a particular course of action. Becker (1961) suggests three sources of side bets. The first source lies in interpersonal relations with regard to one's identity. Here the person has a stake in maintaining a congruent performance as a social actor. A second source of such side bets exists in the everyday interaction patterns that make up a person's life. An example of this is the issue that a man should not change jobs too often or else he might get a reputation as being "unreliable" or "shiftless." Another example is what Becker calls "impersonal bureaucratic arrangements." He illustrates this by showing a teacher who finds she can not leave her present job, because the pension that she accumulated over years will be lost if she does. The third illustration of a side bet is in the process of "individual adjustment to social positions." By working hard at meeting the requirements of a present position, a person may find that he is unable to meet the requirements of another position.

A person is locked into a course of action—committed

—through the process of building up valued relationships that he is unwilling to risk by conducting himself in a way which is inconsistent with these relationships. The past, in effect, feeds present definitions of the situation. Commitments can result from conscious decisions, but very often are made without being realized. These are what Becker calls "commitments by default." The process of routine daily living involves dealing with many trivial, perhaps insignificant, objects when seen by themselves but taken together of such magnitude that the person is unwilling to give them up. There is an increasing valuation placed in acting toward objects in one's world in a consistent manner. The world-taken-for-granted, involving commitments to those realities encountered in the everday life, constitutes the basic "stuff" of social existence. The point Becker is making is clear and significant and relates to other earlier discussions. The nature of collective activity involves persons followings lines of action for reasons which are often independent of the activity itself. Viewing commitment as a process of persons making side bets with themselves, puts the dynamics at the core of situated activity in which social living is seen as ongoing process.

The second concept to be considered here is that of a career. The recognition of a career development in the life of a runaway is essential for understanding the situational meaning of that designation. A career can be defined as a sequence of movements from one position to another (Becker, 1963, p. 24). The concept has been used extensively in the study of occupational systems (Hughes, 1958; Becker and Strauss, 1956) and in the investigation of deviant activities (Becker, 1963; Goffman, 1961a). A major attribute of the career model is that it accounts for a sequence of events which contribute to a certain pattern of behavior. For example, in the Becker (1963) discussion of marijuana use, the focus is on each of the steps someone goes through in order to become a "full fledged" marijuana user (p. 41). Here the pattern of behavior identified as marijuana use is explained by following the sequence of events which eventually changes the individual's behavior and perspective concerning marijuana use. The career model is typically seen to contain a number of stages. These stages represent a progressive growth in the overall development of the career. For example.

Becker (1963) has defined specific steps that characterize the deviant career path, namely, the commission of an act or casual experimentation, the development of deviant motives and interest, getting caught, or being labeled. Interwoven into these stages are the day-to-day contingencies which give shape and direction to career development. In Becker's (1963) words, the notion of career contingency refers to:

> . . .those factors on which mobility from one position to another depends, and includes:
>
> . . .both objective facts of social structure and changes in the perspectives, motivations and desires of the individual. (p. 24)

As both career and commitment apply to the present investigation, they make certain understandings possible. They provide a background to which meaning can be understood or recognized as occurring, (i.e., situationally unfolding among actors). Also, they lend themselves to including structural variables in an examination of why action is taking place or not taking place by the use of career contingencies. Contingencies need be seen not as in process only but also as structural dimensions, as, for example, when one individual has clearly more power over another.

CHAPTER FOOTNOTES

[1]For an in-depth discussion of role passages, identities and the relinquishment of roles, see L. San Giovanni, *Ex-Nuns*, Ablex Publishing, Norwood, New Jersey, 1977.

CHAPTER IV

RESEARCH OVERVIEW

I first became involved with the issue of youth runaways while serving as Director of Research at the New York City Youth Board. Runaway, homeless and throwaway children[1] represented a major public concern of the New York City Youth Board.

At that time, I was completing a survey of youth needs and was approached by my Executive Director concerning the need for basic information about runaways. Since the 1976 Democratic National Convention was scheduled for New York City, an influx of "runaways" was expected, bringing with them a host of problems. The Youth Board felt that the best way to plan services for such a development was to compile basic information about such people. In response to this request, I reviewed earlier investigations of runaway behavior.

These experiences were most helpful in approaching the problem, as well as highly strategic to the present investigation. Visits and conversations with specialists working the field made me familiar with the types of services, shortage of services, and obstacles to services that young persons away from home experience. Contacts with law enforcement officials exposed me to the types of dilemmas faced daily by those attempting to help and police at the same time. Exposure to the variety of statutes and policies provided me a reasonable hold on the "crazyquilt" attitudes characteristic of the runaway scene.[2] Finally, the opportunity to speak with several young people on the run put me in touch with the day-to-day events and descriptions which made up the runaway lifestyle. These events and descriptions were strikingly similar to those experienced by the young drug addicts I had worked with five years earlier in a large urban area.[3] My continued conversations with the youths eventually allowed me to mobilize my thoughts and draft my ideas into a statement of the problem and a research design.

Much of my attention was focused on what was termed the "permission base" of a family. That is, I viewed the issue of running away as a product of how a family organized itself as a group. Families varied in the amount of time, interest and concern they delegated to each other. These dimensions comprised the permission base. It was hypothesized that families characterized as having "tight" permission bases were more likely to define absence as a case of running away than those characterized as having "loose" permission bases. Families with tight organization could not tolerate member absence.

Although this concept was received fairly well by my superiors, it presented several critical problems. First, any empirical verification process would require responses from a young person's family. Since many children away from home strive for anonymity, the possibility of reaching their family was a remote one. Second, this concept placed significant importance on events located in the home (e.g., in the family) yet events out of the home were the more important determinant in staying away from home.

For the next twelve months, my interests were limited to numerous discussions with both youth and runaway specialists concerning my most recent design revisions, the possibility of developing a runaway sample, and the renewed public interest in the topic.

Thereafter, I sought support from the United States Department of Justice Law Enforcement Assistance Administration. However, my application was rejected in April, 1977. This development prompted me to ask the support directly of New York State, and I was put in contact with the Institute of Juvenile Justice. Although support from the Institute was not rendered in the form of a grant, many organizations became cooperative upon hearing about my affiliation with the Juvenile Justice Institute.

The Selection of a Qualitative Research Design

The methodology used in this investigation resembles a "triangulated" (Denzin, 1970:320) approach (Glaser and Strauss, 1968). Using a triangulated approach, the investigation maintains an appreciation and respect for the ties which exist between theory, research problem and method. Rather than rely on a preconceived set of research methods, I used a variety of information-gathering devices which fit the research problem and its setting. Using this approach, my assumption was that no single method is generally superior to another, but rather, to quote Denzin (1970:298), ". . .[methods] are lines of action. . .which will reveal different aspects of a phenomena, depending upon how [each] method is approached, held and acted toward."

As I began this inquiry, no particular set of hypotheses were entertained about runaways. I wished to provide a clear, subjective account of how young people viewed themselves away from their home, and highlight the sometime contradictory events which permeate the lives of children out of their homes. The overall intent of this study was to provide description and exploration rather than hypotheses testing (Riley, 1963:14). Testing of hypotheses about runaways has clearly provided ideas which lack strong exploratory insights and has done so in a premature fashion.

In this study, I used interviews of young people away from home when it was called for; observation when it was possible; and secondary data when available. Each of these methods supplemented the other and provided a perspective distinct from the others.

This has been intensively described by Lofland (1973: 203) in his contrasting of quantitative versus qualitative research objectives. Lofland suggests that qualitative analysis should demonstrate and focus on "what are the characteristics of a social phenomenon, the forms and variations it displays, rather than seek out its causes or the consequences of its presence."

I suggest this statement is an ideal, since each of these tasks tend to overlap each other in the research act. Lofland's concern for "things going on" in the situation under study, and the forms and variations we can identify, more resemble this investigation than do the more rigorously controlled methodologies governed by a "positivist" or "cooperative" model of society.

Defining a Research Population — The Sample

The need for the investigation developed out of my rejection of existing concepts concerning the definition of a runaway. In general, existing studies have lacked a subjective accounting by runaways themselves. Thus the task is to establish what it means to be a runaway and to elicit some understanding about the experience. In studying this issue, no set definition could be relied upon but rather had to be created from the cumulative encounters with young persons themselves.

In the process of constructing the sample for this investigation, I was guided by the position of Schatzman and Strauss (1973:35) regarding the development of "social maps." The creation of such maps allowed both an orientation to the research locale as well as a systematic method to set boundaries and gain organization. My initial mapping steps were similar to those characterized by Schutzman and Strauss (1973:35) where they note:

> The researcher undertakes a mapping operation, moving among the various locales he knows of, listening for evidence of still others, and visiting most or all of these. This is a tour of limited discovery — a first reliable and extensive (not intensive) look at the things, persons, and activities that constitute the site.

Much of this activity was shaped by my previous exposures to the topic, and by my contact person and former colleague who helped me meet people and gain entry into different settings. This gradual process allowed me to develop a sense of "breakpoint" in the daily routines of runaways. The notion of breakpoint was relevant in trying to map out a typical runaway experience. For example, any major shift in daily youth experience, (*i.e., from a friend's home to a program*) was considered a breakpoint and worthy of more attention.

For example, I recognized that young people run within New York City as well as to New York City. This concept allowed me to seek out young people of various types: those who were residents of New York City and those who reported running here from elsewhere. In addition, my exposure to runaway programs and services allowed me to recognize a number of young people in need of such services, and those who were not, and finally, those who had experienced court and those who had not. In broad terms, this mapping process enabled me to tentatively view young people as falling into one of the following four categories: (1) New York children involved in runaway programs; (2) out-of-state children involved in runaway programs; (3) New York children not involved in runaway programs; and (4) out-of-state children not involved in runaway programs.

Although this would by necessity change, it still pointed me towards setting some cognitive limits and gave me a way to evaluate and change the shape of my sample as I continued to meet new respondents.

My initial respondents were young persons involved in the family court and thus, by definition, program-involved and New York City residents. Our conversations suggested that there were other young persons to be met, some older, some from out-of-town and all different from the people spoken to up to this point. This confirmed my original map and I proceeded to seek out such young people to make my sample more complete.

After contacting young people involved in programs, I then began to make limited contact with a wide range of friends.[4] This provided me with a revised perspective on running away, since I came to discover that at one time or another most youth out of home have exposure to runaway services (especially young people who were placed in long term "institutional care" group homes, residence, varieties of foster care, state agencies, etc.). Thus, it became necessary that I not only speak to youth with short-term contact in programs but also that I concentrate on youths reporting very little or very great amounts of time in such programs, since program involvement appeared to affect absence.[5]

The process of developing a sample was an on-going one and I continued to follow leads and compare each respondent in terms of what they told me until few new pieces of information appeared. This process resembles what Polsky (1967) has described as "snowballing." I depended greatly upon a continual monitoring of respondent biographical data in deciding how much my sample mirrored the world

45

of runaways. Further, I continued to keep a close vigil with my contact so that he could double-check and look closely at cases which simply did not correspond to his many years of understanding and information about New York City and its homeless youth scene. This prevented me from searching for or being lead astray by cases that were so atypical that they had no relationship to the problems under investigation.

This brings me to a final point regarding the issue of samples, beyond selection. Because my problem centered on becoming or defining one's self in the runaway role, it was essential that I locate persons with varying amounts of time away from home.[6] It was important that I "constantly compare" (Glaser and Strauss, 1968) respondents in this dimension, while I later compared them with other dimensions viewed as modifiers to the runaway career. To accomplish this, I had to explore the relationship between continued absence and an ever-expanding ability to run away. Finally, as I moved back and forth between my sample data, my map and my research problem, I was aware of the problem of entry obstacles. Although I was free and able to monitor those with whom I had spoken and/or those with whom I needed to speak, I was not able simply to go out and speak with respondents. As I mentioned earlier, some programs refused to give me access to young people. I failed, therefore, to strike up a research bargain (Geer, 1964) and had to "wait out" or look elsewhere for sample respondents. This process eventually prevented me from including everyone in every situation that I believed would be important to completing this investigation.

Locating and Making Contact

Prior to entering the field, my intention was to interview young people involved in family court proceedings because of their continued absence from home. My access to such individuals was through the unofficial cooperation of a family court worker. However, this procedure was only partially successful, since respondents interviewed through these means were mostly young, black, male and distinct from the sorts of persons described in our interviews.

As it became clear that a sample of family court petitions would provide only a partial picture, my attention turned to runaway youth programs. A variety of people from different geographic locations, incomes, ages and races went to runaway programs for help and this factor represented a partial solution to the problem of finding and contacting different populations of runaways. However, the reluctance on the part of programs themselves to provide access to clients prompted me to go to a third source: law enforcement authorities.

In New York City, there are two principal law enforcement units responsible for youth on the run. One is the police runaway unit, an arm of the New York City Police Department. Their jurisdiction stretches across all of New York City and they normally work particular "hot spots" for runaways (runaways turned prostitutes and youth hangouts; e.g., Delancy Street area, Times Square). The second is the Port Authority Runaway Unit. This group is located in the upper level of the New York City Port Authority, and they represent an arm of the Port Authority Police. Their jurisdiction included the main points of entry into New York City; that is, the bus terminal, Grand Central, Penn Station and the airports. Both units deal with diverse types of young people out of their homes and both groups were sensitive to my effort. Two problems exist that impeded my opportunity to speak with youth—age and safety.

Regarding age, youths under sixteen stopped by police are considered minors and communication with them can only be conducted with parental consent. This, for the most part, was logistically impossible. Thus, I could not legitimately speak with detainees. Regarding safety, people over sixteen, if detained on a warrant, might be considered prisoners (in the legal sense). Consequently, police have a responsibility to insure their safe delivery to court. Moreover, they must always insure the safety of "civilians" vis-a-vis their charges. Both these issues were understandable, even from my vantage point.

Bracey (1977) reported similar problems in attempting to deal with juvenile prostitutes.

This last set of developments prompted me to obtain a fourth source of contacts—the youths themselves. Having already made several contacts among young people involved in family court and runaway programs, I was able to maintain a regular dialogue with two youths. Both were curious about my interests and both were in need of the attention my investigation was focusing on them. Through my family court contact, we continued to meet on different occasions. At my request, they brought friends to our meetings — people similar to themselves and doing the same thing as they were.[7] This outcome proved helpful to the investigation since it opened up the possibility of reaching young people without having to depend on programs.

At the time, I thought this method had another advantage, because these were people not known to the authorities. Thus, there would be the possibility of a broader sample. However, I recognized that even these young people periodically had the need for a service provided by a runaway program.

Field Contacts

Two regular contact persons were relied upon in the course of this investigation. Both these contacts have been mentioned previously in this section. Both these individuals were known to me before I began this investigation; one having worked with me in my prior position as a youth gang worker. They assisted me in locating, contacting, verifying and gaining entry to runaway settings. In addition, both spent numerous hours in conversation with me and reviewed many of the ideas I espoused during the course of this effort. Both helped me set up meetings with young people and both helped vouch for my purposes and interests in doing this study. Finally, both my field contacts served to strain pieces of information that I didn't understand or were conceptually vague. My continued access and discussion with these individuals insured a level of reliability that would not have been possible considering the demands of the interviewing settings, the suspicions of some of the young people, and the nature of the problem itself.

Research Obstacles

As suggested by Schatzman and Strauss (1973), the notion of doing field work "conjures up all sorts of images and ideas in the minds of onlookers" (p.2). Beyond this, I found that it also conjures up all sorts of obstacles. In conducting my investigation on runaways, I encountered a host of very frustrating problems. Although it would be impossible and somewhat unnecessary to mention them all, I should like to comment here on the ones which had the most logistical influence on gathering the data.

Program Suspicions

A very serious problem encountered in the initial stages of this investigation was the general suspicions of youth runaway programs about the nature of my work. These suspicions were encountered, despite the fact that I elaborated on prior experience in the field and offered to share my findings with each program.[8] The suspicions were based upon two types of concerns held by programs. First, a majority of the programs serving runaways feared for the welfare and privacy of their clients. Many claimed to have taken part in prior investigations and, as a result, experienced invasions of privacy, interruptions of services and daily program routines, misuse of data and a general "swelled head" phenomena among the clients being continually interviewed. For example, one program director reported to me that she received about 70 calls a day that requested permission to study the program, causing an almost impossible situation.[9] Second, a number of programs feared the effect of such an effort on funding. Many directors feel that outside scrutiny of performance can influence funding decisions because programs are, to some degree, in competition for similar dollars. Therefore, passing on too much information can create problems.

This combination of factors presented consequences for this investigation since it blocked one source of potential respondents and forced me to look elsewhere for youth on the run. Looking elsewhere proved to be enlightening, since I quickly recognized that, although a young person may not presently be involved in a runaway service, sooner or later some type of service becomes important to most youth.

For example, Kevin, age 17, was introduced to me through a resident of a Lower East Side runaway program. Kevin was not living at the runaway center at the time we spoke, however. After intensive conversations with Kevin, I learned that he often used programs in between jobs or when his luck was running bad. This type of response occurred over and over again and prompted me to explore the relationship between runaway programs and becoming a runaway.

The Research Situation as an Awkward Encounter

I thought of this investigation as an encounter between myself and a variety of young people no longer living at home. As with all social encounters, a setting must exist within which the encounter can unfold. Conducting research in this investigation, I passed through a number of settings and some were more uncomfortable than others. It is the uncomfortable setting that I wish to briefly reflect on since this setting was most threatening to my effort.

Meeting young runaways for research purposes occurred in a number of places. I met members of my sample in three parks, one school, numerous storefronts (programs), Kennedy Airport, the Port Authority, a car wash, a hallway, Manhattan Family Court, the beach, one discotheque, several neighborhood bars, a social club, two YMCA's and dozens of fast food places (circa Burger King and White Castle). I found the Burger King settings the easiest to work in and the least awkward and the storefronts the hardest. I say this because I found that I had a legitimate reason to be at a fast food place and there were plenty of props like coffee and food. The anonymous atmosphere was helpful and neither I nor my respondents felt strained.[10] In this type of setting, we were in full view of each other as well as everyone else and yet we knew no one and no one knew us. The interview flowed well with us both relaxed.

This was not the case in the storefront program settings. Here, I felt awkward, I felt alien and a visitor, and perceived the same sort of feeling among respondents attempting to be cool and complacent among peers. I suspect that several young people felt as if they were perceived to be more privileged than others, engaged in dialogue with a visitor, while others simply "hang out," waiting for either their chance (if they volunteered), phone calls, lunch, a string of good luck or anything else to deliver them to another setting. The conversations in these settings were superficial. I felt little was being said yet it was taking all day to say it! Furthermore, I was less compelled to probe and dig for different items in each encounter.[11]

These experiences prompted me to avoid the "quasi-captive" audiences found in runaway programs and push for interviews in public settings (i.e., fast food places). This proved helpful and not at all awkward since these settings were usually in a convenient area and most respondents, as well as my contact, enjoyed the option of having something to eat.

Further, when more than one respondent showed up, the encounter was more of an open discussion than an interview, something which is not at all awkward in fast food settings.

Beyond the perception of the awkwardness issue, several other dimensions appear to be worth mentioning as they either contribute or modify awkwardness; these include, danger, color/race and sex.

Potential Danger

Potential danger was a quality which was present during the course of this investigation. The presence of danger sometimes rendered me ineffective since I was preoccupied with the idea of being ripped off by other than the respondents (i.e., rivals, stick-up types, etc.) in the more remote settings. Being "set up" by the respondents themselves for whatever reason they might have had to do so, or being implicated or arrested by the police in connection with persons or events in which I was having my contacts was another concern.[12] With respect to race and color, I found myself at a real disadvantage in black and Puerto Rican neighborhoods. Because I worked in these settings in the past as a street worker, I normally found myself at ease in areas such as East New York and East Harlem. My use of a contact or go-between (a colleague) was not a great deal of help since he rarely stayed the entire interview. I attribute this experience, in part, to my role as researcher, having been identified as such, and, in part, to a polarization I have recognized more than ever as existing between blacks and whites.

Phrases such as "it's different for white folks" entered our dialogue regularly and it was both difficult and awkward for me to keep my being white out of the conversation. Further, I feel some of the respondents held back feelings because of racial differences.[13] Finally, since some items generated hostile feelings—for example, seeking work rather than some other less legitimate means of support—I found myself steering clear of these items, rather than jeopardizing the entire interview encounter.

A third area which I viewed as a detriment to the entire process was that of sex. When my respondents were female, the situations proved to be difficult. Obviously, some interviews went much better than others. However, with women respondents, my subjective feeling was that some information was lost.

For example, several opportunities to speak with women respondents occurred in the presence of their boyfriends, or those who might be sociologically viewed as their protectors. This type of encounter made it difficult to probe and explore items which might challenge the emotional stake these persons had for each other and, thus, produced a loss of data. Further, such a probe could have been mistaken for an intrusion on my part and would thus, again, bring threatening feelings to the setting.

Finally, I think several of the women respondents felt compelled to impress me with how independent and capable they were. Consequently, as a male, my challenges or probes were received by even further talking around the issue on their part.

Interviews, Observations and Available Program Records

In this investigation, there were essentially three methods used in collecting data: (1) interviews, (2) observations and (3) existing records. Interviews contributed the greatest amount of information but the first-hand observations and records provided invaluable insights and made the interviews even stronger. In some cases, the three methods were used in tandem and served as checks upon the others and, in some cases, each method served as a sole and primary data source.

The Interviews

As I suggested above, I have viewed my contacts with young people as encounters. This was especially true in the interviews where both myself and the respondent were exchanging ideas, and where I was initiating (Kassenbaum, 1970, p. 132), and controlling the interview topics.

Many of my interviews were formal, in the sense that I had to set up appointments, my interview guide was used and I would take notes. These types of interviews comprise the bulk of the data in this study. However, other interviews were very casual and non-directed,[14] and took place at fast food places, parks, bars and discos. At the park, I would take the role of an interested colleague, this stance being possible only when my contact and former fellow worker was present. When he was not, I tried to maintain the interview by merely keeping the conversation going. If the conversation shifted to another topic, so did I. These interviews resemble the kinds of situations described by Donald Roy (1970) as "continuous interviewing while observing," in his studies of southern labor unions (pp. 216-244). A total of 36 interviews were collected in this effort. Approximately 18 took place in fast food settings within New York City. The average duration of each interview was about one hour, but they ranged from approximately 30 minutes to two hours. Nine of the 36 individuals met with me on five separate occasions beyond the original interview.

Within each interview encounter, I explained that I was doing a preliminary investigation on youth lifestyles in New York City and, in particular, independent lifestyles. I noted that both the respondent's peers and my contact (when present) thought they would be excellent sources to speak with on the runaway subject.

Only one person refused to engage in discussion, yet we did talk about other issues related to this topic. Generally, I tried to take as few notes as possible in order to maintain a conversational atmosphere.[15] However, in several instances, note-taking upset respondents and, at my offering, I ceased to do so. Except in those few instances characterized above as awkward, I submit that each interview encounter allowed me to take away an amount of information equal to my expectations.

With respect to specific techniques used, there were basically two styles used in the process of interviewing. The first concerned itself with controlling the order of the questions into sections (see schedule in Appendix X). Thus, all questions dealing with the possibility of returning home were grouped together. This interview form resembles what Merton and Kendall (1946) call a focused interview (pp. 541-552) and is very similar to that used by Becker, Geer, et. al (1961, p. 29) in their study of medical student life.

When a respondent brought up a topic which was out of sequence, I attempted to follow it up immediately, a technique relied upon by Dalton (1967, p. 82). In doing so, I learned that portions of some interview topics might be summarized. When this occurred, questioning became natural and I began to ignore the interview guide. This procedure was used until the conclusion of the interview—unless, of course, a respondent volunteered additional information.

The second interviewing tactic involved my use of the following concluding question: "Based on what we have talked about, how well could I describe your experiences to date?" This question was designed to obtain an assessment regarding the adequacy of the interview as well as to stimulate further discussion about being away. In practice, only the most vocal and interested seemed to make further comment. Those whom I felt weren't involved in the encounter simply said nothing.

A final note on the topic of interviews has to do with the use of probe (Polsky, 1967). A probe is defined as an interview device used to explore specific issues in more detail. Through each of my interviews, I relied heavily on probes to explore areas that needed further detail and clarification. To the extent that they became a regular part of my behavior, I no longer view them as a separate topic. However, they were used on a regular basis in this investigation.

Interview Schedule

The development of the interview schedule (see Appendix 1) came as a direct result of preliminary responses gathered in the field. My original schedule was administered to a total of eleven respondents. It contained four sections or areas dealing with:

1. Biographical information
2. Respondent's present situation
3. Shifts in respondent situation
4. Returning home issues

Within each section was a set of questions dealing specifically with particular information. For example, under the section on a respondent's present situation, there were questions on residence, financial and emotional support, and a group of follow-up short items, such as residence (with whom, what and where). As field work continued, the original schedule proved to be too bulky and too constraining. In response, some items were dropped. In addition, some respondents answered questions out of turn and others fell into a conversational pattern, thus causing me to change my tactics as needed.

I found that I did not have to ask each of the questions contained in my original questionnaire, but only lead the conversation and the issues would eventually be covered.[16] The final product contained approximately 30 percent fewer items. However, it included the four original sections mentioned above.

Runaway Program Interviews

In addition to the interviews conducted with youth located out of their homes, I completed a total of 17 interviews with adult representatives of 17 runaway programs.

The topics covered in this interview schedule included program philosophy regarding runaways, types of services offered, history of project, exploration of client problems as they concern remaining away versus returning home, discussions of intake criteria and program follow-up, discussion of typical "case," and the relationship of visited programs to other similar projects. Interviews were undertaken in a total of eight counties within a radius of approximately ninety miles from New York City. The specific counties included:

New York	Staten Island
Queens	Nassau
The Bronx	Suffolk
	Bergen (New Jersey)

The program director, supervisor or administrator was the individual within the agency I questioned.[17] The program representatives were for the most part cooperative and several projects accommodated me to the extent of providing me with intake and client data.

Observations

I spent a total of approximately 70 hours engaged in observation. As discussed earlier, my interviews took place in a variety of contexts. Likewise, my observations occurred in many places, since they grew from the interview circumstances. But in a minor number of cases, scheduling of interviews through the assistance of my contact proved futile. Young people either failed to show up, dropped out and left runaway programs or, in one case, refused to talk. To fill this time and capitalize on the presence of my contact, I accompanied him on a number of his own field encounters.[18] This practice enabled me to venture forth into some more natural settings, putting aside my usual responsibilities. Within these settings I observed as much as possible. However, I was also trying to be sincere, sociable and concerned. As a result, I found these contacts somewhat different. However, much similar to the experience of Herbert Gans (1968),[19] I felt myself to be "psychologically on the margins" of such encounters (p. 304). Despite this feeling, I was exposed to a number of activities which might not have been possible without my entering into an observer role.

For example, independent of conducting interviews, I was able to simply visit and observe regular nightspots in which I learned how runaways hustle unsuspecting patrons on behalf of increasing their fortunes. Also, I was able to vary my observations to the degree that I was present on weekdays versus weekends and was able to observe pre-twelve AM versus post-twelve AM behavior, and hot weather versus cold weather needs of runaways.

Available Records

Several projects, upon my request, allowed me to view different records about client intake, sources of referral and field reports, written on behalf of anonymous clients concerning their future plans regarding shelter, returning home and similar issues. Similar to my observations, this type of data verified or strengthened the picture that was emerging in the investigation. For example, one project kept records on the circumstances clients reported as the major reason for leaving home. By comparing these pieces of information with the pieces I collected from my respondents, I was able to gauge how similar or dissimilar these experiences were to the ones reported in the programs. Moreover, program records appeared to be a more reliable source of data on issues like the amount of time spent in programs, since most runaway program reporting and funding requirements demanded that such detail be provided.

Finally, having a third source of data provided me with several leads and insights on how runaways get to find out about runaway programs. For example, although in a minority, some people did not find out about runaway services through the advice of friends but rather under the direction of caseworkers at the Department of Social Services.

Organization of Data and Analysis[20]

The research focus of this book, as discussed earlier, is the process and behavioral stages through which someone eventually acquires a runaway identity and perspective. Consequently, the research method used devotes its analytic energies toward the interaction among runaways that develops such an identity and perspective. This section details the steps that comprised the analytic phase of my work.

The initial step in my analytic efforts was to orient myself to the task of collecting data that corresponded to the goals of this study. In practice, this process required several activities, all preparatory in nature.

First, I continually reminded myself not to foreclose on any piece of data. As new pieces of data came in, I systematically accommodated them into my existing notes. Second, I physically set up a system of data collection that reflected the aims of my investigation, yet was flexible enough to adjust to changes if experienced in the field.

My collection strategy consisted of a set of three special notebooks, each containing different but interrelated pieces of data. Book One contained interviews with young people and runaway program workers. Book Two contained my notes and descriptions of different places I had visited. Book Three contained my reflections, field contact reflections, leads and theory insights that I had been making about Books One and Two. Consequently, as I continued to collect data in Book One, my notes (Book Two) and insights (Books Two and Three) matured.

When I became more and more familiar with a specific runaway theme or idea (via continual interviewing and rereading of interviews), I cross-referenced each of the three books to each other. This highlighted the importance of the particular area which emerged when a new interview was obtained. I checked its context against its area and either fit it into a pre-existing topic or began a new area.

Using this continual reference to each of the three books, I was able to blend information gathered through discussion (interviews), Book One; observation (field contacts and myself), Book Two; and my theoretical insight, Book Three. For example, one issue I gathered continual data on was the "limited contact with home syndrome." I found, in talking with some young people, that there was a constant need or intent to contact home. My original interviews contained information on this need and at the time hypothesized that it was a means to insure support. However, as interviews proceeded, I noted in both my observations and in my discussions with field contacts (Book Two), that the young people least in need of support were those who were most interested in making home contacts. These two separate observations or pieces of data might appear at first to be at odds, and in no way worthy of integration. Yet my feelings were that they were related. As such, my collection system did not dispose of this issue but simply flagged it until I could explore the issue further in a subsequent interview. When I did, I discovered that some young people contact home to demonstrate that they have made it—that they would come home but don't need to anymore. . .and they were no longer the same person everyone knew! Consequently, I discovered that for some runaways a liaison with home had little to do with support but rather was a demonstration to parents that they could take or leave their role as a son or daughter. They gained a satisfaction from this because it was the role of a son or daughter which was often reported as problematic by the young person. No longer having to perform in this role gave the young person a sense of freedom from their problems.

The insight and direction in developing this theory came from Notebook Three, which contained a number of analytic categories that I had put together as I continued to collect data. One analytic category was role performance (Goffman, 1961). I used this category to explore the matter mentioned above in later discussions and in interpreting the responses given on why people contact home when they really don't need to.

My third step was to separate each of the interview responses as they were gathered with my schedule and recorded in Book One. This process included making outline copies of each respondent interview and then putting them into area envelopes. I placed each of my responses into area envelopes after I inspected the content and judged that a set of questions and responses belonged in an area. In some cases, I included more than one question in an area envelope. For example, responses found in my means of support envelope usually included responses to family contacts, issues, the basis for finding out about agencies, the pitfalls of seeking out support, etc. Because each of these items corresponded to the theme of "support" they became categorized as such.

My fourth step was to draw up a set of finalized theoretical and grounded concepts. These concepts were formed from many of the responses that were lumped into my area envelopes. My final list was based upon insights I have developed in Notebook Three. This process of finalizing included the original ideas put forth when I began this effort and also those developed after I entered the field. As such, I submit that the conceptual basis for my analysis has been grounded in the everyday events of these runaways I encountered in the field. Not all items in the final set of concepts were used in this investigation.[21] As I moved between what I included in my area envelopes and what I depended upon as a conceptual frame of reference, some items became essential while others became extraneous. I kept a list of my important concepts and modified it on an ongoing basis.

The last step in my analytic effort was to develop an overview or typology of runaway careers. My purpose in doing so was to arrange my information in a way that would make it most understandable to the reader, especially as it related to the process of becoming a runaway. Further, I clearly linked my available data about runaways to the major theoretical concepts developed in this study. In a sense, I was fitting my data with my concepts.

A guiding perspective in this effort was Becker's (1940) notion of a "constructed type." "Constructed types," in contrast to other typifications, became constructed by the researcher, based upon some theory, concern, description or empirical observation and they became abstracted into an idealized form. For my purposes, I felt the need to explain both discrepancies and information discovered in the runaway definition process, without abandoning the conceptual background that emerged in this investigation. Using typology, I was able to fit my observation about runaways with my conceptual background and afterward place both into a type that accounted for variation and differences along a continuum.

For example, a major assumption of this investigation is that a runaway role is learned over a period of time. Following my data in the form of both core cases; i.e., persons seen more than once and one-time interviews, I identified different styles of learning the role. I refer to these (see Chapter I) as aggressive, passive and indifferent. Each represents different qualities with respect to how persons mark off role requirements, territories, friendships, etc. Further, each is based upon observation. I became more confident that I could fit them into the notion of a runaway career. Similarly, I became aware that each affected the runaway career. I continued to modify data until I reached the point where I felt that each of the major variations observed had been accounted for using a type and that each had been related to the problem of becoming a runaway. This process was repeated many times in an attempt to match my observations with my analysis. This was, in general, the way I was able to identify themes like hustling, the decision to leave home and how these concerns are related to the career. Likewise, in developing frequency data on respondents, I separated respondents into categories and counted.

These systems formed the basis of my research methodology. They successfully allowed data-gathering, organization and expansion of records as new information became available and highlighted previous perceptions.

CHAPTER FOOTNOTES

[1]Theodore Hackman (1977) has discussed the issues of throwaways and homeless versus runaway youth in his investigation of *Homeless Youth*. Such distinctions are important to our topic discussion to the extent that youth view themselves as one designation rather than another. During this investigation, throwaways or homeless youth were identified by the fact that they were either (1) asked

to leave by parents or (2) reported to a home setting to which they could not return. This is in contrast with having youth runaways who reported themselves as linked to regular routines and little interest to return home.

[2]This crazy-quilt pattern is exemplified in the varied home rule requirements used in determining if someone is away. For example, in New York State, a young person may be considered a runaway if he or she is below the age of 16 and is without visible means of support or shelter. This same young person, if a former resident in a state which uses 18 as the minimum age, is immune from police jurisdiction and cannot be held under New York State Law (See Chapter I).

[3]During 1970-71, I worked as a youth worker with a popular youth advocate agency in a large urban area. During this time I became familiar with the sorts of problems drug abusers reported, such as obtaining methodine (it wasn't yet popular), avoiding police, the need to reduce the costs of habits, being set up by friends, finding a means of support, and generally getting one's family to understand the difficulty of being addicted to drugs.

[4]This tactic was originally suggested to me by my field contact who, in many cases, had earlier experiences dealing with many of the clients' peers. He suggested that both their curiosity and eventual cooperation might enhance my efforts.

[5]This process of constantly comparing "variables" as exhibited by young persons themselves (i.e., court involved not court involved) allowed for the opportunity to build a more representative base from which to discuss and explore what it means to be a runaway.

[6]As a heuristic device, I used weeks, months and years as the basis upon which to assign someone into a short, medium or long amount of time away from home. For example, if a respondent described him or herself in terms of days or weeks, I considered this a short time away from home. In contrast, others might (and did) describe themselves in terms of years away. In either case, it is the respondent who is locating himself with respect to amount of time away from home, rather than the researcher.

[7]Indirectly, this process served as a reliability check on the information collected, since several of the people spoken to either *corrected* or *challenged* some of the state-

ments made by other young people in their presence. This served to "screen" out some of the "extreme" stories of dubious nature.

[8]This practice most closely resembles that procedure referred to by Geer as striking up a "research bargain" (in Hammond, [1964]). Schatzman and Strauss have also commented on this practice, suggesting that the ability to provide information to those studied puts the researcher in a better position with respect to receiving "cooperation." (See Chapter 2 in *Field Work*, Leonard Schatzman and Anselm Strauss.)

[9]I found this claim to be a bit "inflated" based upon the fact that if a program were to receive 70 calls a day, five days a week, for fifty-two weeks a year, that would make a total of 18,200 calls to the program.

[10]I use the term "friend" here since I became close with one of the respondents to the point where we would discuss issues, share advice, problems, etc., beyond the research problem. This development made me more sensitive to the manner in which I disengaged from the field setting.

[11]It becomes difficult to gather information on "future plans" or feelings about one's predicament in the near presence of program staff. I say this because the programs view themselves as partly instrumental in the change and/or limited salvation of the runaway. Thus, the young person who recognizes this often feels a certain allegiance to the program and views it as good rather than something less than good.

[12]John Irwin has commented in length about this problem, especially in response to the Polsky position of needing to "remain" in the natural setting you study. Irwin contends that this can not only be awkward but also dangerous to a naive researcher who is mistaken for one of the group he is studying, as in the case of mass arrests or violence. (For further discussion, see Jack Douglas, *Research on Deviance*, Random House, 1974.)

[13]I don't mean to imply that racial differences between researcher and respondents are a new or unusual problem, but only that the everyday feelings of this particular group of people, (out of home, out of work, out of money, etc.) makes issues like hostility, deference, and indifference in the interview setting very real, and things that need to be contended with.

[14]For two in-depth discussions on forms and varieties of interviews as well as the strategies which can be used with them on behalf of collecting data, see Richardson, Stephen A., Barbara S. Dohrenwend, and D. Klein, *Interviewing, Its Form and Functions*. New York: Basic Books, Inc., 1965 and Gordon, Raymond L., *Interviewing Strategy, Techniques and Tactics*. Homewood, IL: The Dorsey Press, 1969.

[15]As a regular practice, I rewrote my interviews within two hours after having spoken to an individual. This was done to primarily avoid the problem of recall. Also, this was especially done in those cases where I could not write in a respondent's presence. However, in some cases, it proved to be nearly impossible to remain on this schedule.

[16]Specific "buzz" items appeared to surface as interviewing continued. For example, when I would cover the issue of court and its influence on runaway decision-making (under problems), an inevitable topic that surfaced was the warrant. Warrants are often drawn on people under 16 in connection with their absence from home. If a person does get intercepted by police, the presence of a warrant provides a grounds for being held.

[17]In every case, it was only the director, supervisor or administrator who would take the role. Few, if any, "line-staff" were interested in taking on such a responsibility, until the director first did so.

[18]Part of my contact's responsibility was to locate and counsel young people in and around their neighborhood or local "hang-out" while they continued their absence from home.

[19]For a further discussion on "styles" in field research encounters, see Beck, Bernard, "Cooking Welfare Stew," in Robert W. Habenstein, *Pathways to Data: Field Methods for Studying Ongoing Social Organizations*, Chicago: Aldine Publishing Co., 1968.

[20]As background discussion and guides to my analysis, I consulted the works of John Lofland, *Analyzing Social Settings*, (Chapter 9) and Schatzman and Strauss, *Field Work*, (Chapter 6) and Jacqueline Wiseman, *The Research Web*. Each of these efforts provide details on the "How to," organization and analysis phase of field work.

[21]For example, some of the data selected from pro-

gram records really did not tend to be relevant.

CHAPTER V

Introduction

Adolescence is normally a difficult period in a person's life and the problems that cloud the life of a child away from home are no exception.

The general background of my respondents could also be that of a normal adolescent. In addition, respondents had many typical adolescent modes of expression and ideas. However, there was a pattern that emerged among the children questioned. There were typical events associated with people leaving home, a pattern of occurrences, activities and social relationships that constituted a child's day out of the home, and issues and concerns that were exclusively those of a runaway.

The data that follows describes the general characteristics of the sample group used in this investigation.[1] This background is the foundation that gradually leads a young person from what may start as an outgrowth of adolescent rebellion but eventually becomes a clearly defined runaway role and lifestyle.

Characteristics of Respondent Sample, By Age and Sex

Nearly three quarters of the respondents of this investigation were male (see Table 1) and 83% of the respondents were at least fourteen years of age or older (see Table 2). There were no female respondents below the age of fourteen interviewed in this study. Both fourteen and fifteen year olds made up the bulk of the respondent population.[2]

TABLE 1
ANALYSIS OF RESPONDENTS BY SEX

	Number	Percentage of Total Sample
Male	26	72.2%
Female	20	27.8%
	36	100.0%

TABLE 2
ANALYSIS OF RESPONDENTS BY AGE

Age	Number	Percentage of Total Sample
10	1	2.7%
11	2	5.5%
12	1	2.7%
13	2	5.5%
14	10	28.0%
15	9	25.0%
16	5	14.0%
17	2	5.5%
18	3	8.4%
19	0	0.0%
20	1	2.7%
	36	100.0%

In comparison with other available information, the distribution of age and sex is somewhat different. For example, Hackman, in a 1977 New York City investigation on runaways, reported that his sample included a preponderance of 16 and 17 year olds. However, he noted that the number of 16 and 17 year olds decreased and respondents became younger as he moved toward the "outer" boroughs of New York City (Bronx). The 1976 New York City Youth Board investigation of runaways reported the majority of its respondents to be sixteen years of age or older. However, in that case, the emphasis was on people coming to New York City, as contrasted with native New Yorkers, and they typically proved to be older persons. The age data reported

66

by the 1976 Massachusetts Committee on Children and Youth Study,[3] cited that the onset of absence from home had begun to appear at earlier ages (below sixteen). Furthermore, this response group is similar to those in a 1974 investigation by Brennan (1975) where a national probability sample was used to discover the incidence and frequency of runaway behavior.

The fact that a younger response group surfaced in this study can be explained by its sampling procedure. Because the original response group was drawn from a family court setting, respondents would have to be below sixteen years of age. Moreover, since I later collected and relied on responses from their peers, they were more likely to be about the same age as the respondent. Thus, overall, I collected data on younger children.

Regarding respondent sex, data gathered here shows that 72.2% of my respondents were male and 27.8% were female. This trend follows several other recent investigations conducted on youth away from home.[4] I believe it also mirrors a social-juvenile justice feeling for not wishing to prosecute young women below the age of sixteen unless there is a great deal of pressure from outside that court to do so.

In summary, most respondents were young males, fourteen and fifteen years of age.

Race and Ethnicity

More than 70% of the respondents were either Black or Hispanic. This figure conforms to the figures reported by both the Youth Board and Hackman investigations. It also amplifies the fact that the New York City Juvenile Justice system is, for the most part, dealing with Black and Hispanic youth. Table 3 summarizes the race/ethnicity data gathered.

TABLE 3
ANALYSIS OF RESPONDENTS BY RACE/ETHNICITY

	Number	Percentage of Total Sample
Blacks	15	41.6%
Hispanic	12	33.3%
White	9	25.1%
Other	0	0.0%
	36	100.0%

Native Area of Residence

Eighty-six percent of the young people spoken to were children of families living in New York State, more than 75% of the young people were residents of New York City for at least the last five years. Three were from the neighboring states of New Jersey, Connecticut and Pennsylvania. One respondent was from Washington, D.C. and one from Central America.

Table 4, below, reports on the specific areas from which young people reported coming.

TABLE 4
ANALYSIS OF RESPONDENTS BY NATIVE
AREA OF RESIDENCE

	Number	Percentage
New York City (5 boroughs)	28	77.7%
Nassau, Suffolk, Westchester Area	3	8.3%
New Jersey, Connecticut, Pennsylvania	3	8.3%
Washington, D.C., and Central America	2	5.7%

Reported Reasons Why Youth Left Home

During this investigation, respondents were asked to recount the reasons or circumstances for their leaving home. A vast majority of respondents (77.8%) reported that "problems between themselves and their mother or father" were the reason for leaving. This meant that:

a) they could not keep late hours away from home or stay away overnight

b) they could not associate with persons recognized by parents or siblings as known troublemakers

c) they were not performing well in school

d) they were asking for too much in terms of money, clothing, etc., from parents

e) they were not assuming important family roles assigned to them, or

f) they were beaten.

Not one respondent gave just one reason for problems with parents; young people usually spoke of at least two or three reasons for leaving. In some cases, the issue of leaving was compounded by either conflict with brothers or sisters, parents, the person's boyfriend or girlfriend, surrogate father or other extended family member.

Table 5 below provides specific reasons given why youth feel the need to leave home.

TABLE 5
PRESENTATION OF RESPONDENTS REASONS
FOR LEAVING HOME

Reason	Number	Percentage of Total Sample
A. Problems between self and parent	28	77.8%
B. Pushed out or thrown out of home	3	8.4%
C. Mutual agreement between parent and child	3	8.4%
D. Opportunity to live elsewhere	1	2.7%
E. Don't really know	1	2.7%
	36	100.0%

Beyond the matter of a reason for leaving home, two other related dimensions emerged in the course of this investigation. The first is the number of prior attempts at leaving home. The second is prior family court contact as a result of leaving home. First, regarding prior absence, more than one-half (52.4%) of the respondents reported having been away from home prior to this occasion. Table 6 presents the distribution of prior absence among respondents.

TABLE 6
ANALYSIS OF RESPONDENTS PRIOR ABSENCE
FROM HOME STATEMENTS

	Number	Percentage of Total Sample
Prior Absence	19	52.4%
No Prior Absence	17	47.6%
	36	100.0%

Of the group reporting earlier absence from home, eight out of ten did so at least three times. Several of these youth reported they left from temporary shelters or placement settings which had been ordered by the family court. Second, with respect to court contact, all of the youths with three or more runaway episodes reported that they had been to court in the past because of absence from home.

Each of these pieces of data suggest that some distant connection exists between absence from home, court reaction to absence, and continued absence despite court action. That is, the more the young person's absence made an issue through a court appearance (for the purpose of limiting absence), the greater and more frequent becomes absence. When respondents were cross-examined on the related issues of absence and subsequent court action, most reported that either parents (especially mother), or their school, in cooperation with parents, initiated their first appearance in court.

None of the respondents reported finding any help from the court proceeding. Most reported that once they promised to return home or make adjustments, the issue was dropped. Two persons reported that they were uncertain if they were supposed to return to court; both wished to drop the subject. All of the respondents who had been to court noted that parents were angry with the results achieved at court. Some noted that parents wanted the court to do more than they did. Many youths stated that they were supposed to go to special schools[5] after they returned home. However, many of the respondents reported going only one or two times or when they wanted to. They suggested that parents became even more angry when they caught them in the street instead of being in the court-assigned school. Many felt that if they went back home, they would be sent back to court or would be arrested by police.

Judging from responses gathered through an in-depth probing of youth family court experience, several things can be said about the court. (1) The court serves as a poor device to insure compliance with both schools and parents. This is based upon the observation that respondents did not really understand the need to be in court, or the demands the court was making in response to their alleged problem behavior. This point was especially supported by a comment made by one respondent who had been to court at least seven times:

*Well, you know, like the court won't do any-
thing to you or for your mother but tell you
that you need to listen and do what your
mother says. You know, like when you need
to stay home. You see the judge don't know
you cause he has to talk to a lot of kids. He
tells us all the same thing. Sometimes they send
you to a place that has counselors and programs to help you, but it's no help. You go a
couple of times and you talk about the same
things with the same people. After I go, my
mother ain't mad at me no more, so I don't
need to go to court. I don't know why I had to
go to court, they can't do anything for you.
It's only when my mother is mad.*

Respondent number 17

(2) In the eyes of respondents, once absence from home is
brought to the attention of the court, little is accomplished.
Table 7 provides summary data regarding absence and family
court contact.

TABLE 7
ANALYSIS OF RESPONDENTS TIME
AWAY FROM HOME STATEMENTS

	Number	Percentage of Total Sample
0-6 months	14	38.9%
7-12 months	10	27.7%
13-18 months	8	22.2%
19 months or more	4	11.1%
	36	100.0%

Duration of Absence

The amount of time reported away from home varied
from a minimum of six days to a maximum of four years.[6]
Table 7 provides data on the differing amounts of time reported by young people away from home.

As noted in the table, 38.9% of the sample has been
away from home six months or less. This time category was
most often reported by young people. It should be pointed
out that the question posed to respondents focused on the
most recent absence from home. No earlier absence was con-

71

sidered in the overall amount of time spent away from home. However, when examining the relationship between the amount of absence time reported and the number of previous absences from home, youth with prior absence tend to be out of their home for longer periods.

TABLE 8
COMPARISON OF AMOUNT OF TIME AWAY
FROM HOME BY PRIOR ABSENCE

	None	One or More
0-6 months	14	5
7-12 months	1	5
13-18 months	2	5
19 months or more	0	4
	100%	100%
	(17)	(19)

Living Arrangements

There were three types of living arrangements reported by young people while away from home: friends, extended family contacts and supportive youth shelter programs.

Every person spoken with said friends were used as a means of obtaining residence at least one time. That is, they would either call friends or go to their homes in order to obtain temporary shelter. Friends were typically sought out before family or runaway programs were consulted. In most of my conversations, youth did not report any pre-planning for the assistance of friends. Most young people simply called by telephone, or went directly to a friend's home. Although few spoke of pre-planning, most felt that friends would be familiar with the present predicament and would be sympathetic. The respondents indicated that in most cases, friends do help; however, they are not always in a position to give help, particularly when they are living with their own parents.

The parents of friends are continual or potential obstacles for young persons looking for shelter. In many cases, parents are not informed about the presence of other children, or else young persons using the facilities of friends do so only when friends' parents are at work, out of town, or

72

generally out of the picture. This practice is relied upon because parents do not wish to become involved with other people's problems or they feel this type of experience is a bad one for their own children. These feelings result in the parent refusing refuge despite the apparent need for it.

When I spoke to runaway program personnel about this issue, they generally characterized parents' feelings into three categories. The first was indifference. Here, the parent really has no opinion or interest in what another parent's child does, or for that matter, what their own children do! In such a case, the parent takes little interest in home events, spends little time in the home itself, and generally is not tuned into the home setting enough to care about harboring a homeless young person. The only concern here is to make certain that the outsider doesn't "overstay the stay" or steal anything. In this type of setting, it is not unusual for the host children to be runaways. Thus, absence or presence of children, in general, isn't of very much importance – especially if they are not your own.

A second type of parent represents the other extreme – those who are over concerned and scrutinize everything and everyone in the home. Such parents wish to present clear-cut, conservative lifestyles to their children and harboring someone's child represents a real threat. When the visit is not seen as a threat, it is often seen as an issue of competition. These parents spend large amounts of time with their children and when the appearance and attraction to a friend cuts into that time, the parent finds that he or she must compete against the newcomer. In certain cases, such a reaction can more quickly compel parents into calling the police or punishing their own children under the guise of helping out another parent or not wanting to be held legally responsible. The following case in point was depicted by one program worker when describing circumstances surrounding the arrival of two newcomers in the program.

They were telling me that they were the best of friends and that they both could not return home. When I asked them why they could not return home, one of them told me that she would be beaten! When I inquired why, she said because her mother was pissed that her

*friend was staying in their house. At that
point, the other girl chimed in and said that
she was living at different friends' homes
since she ran away. She said that she was
sorry it was causing all this trouble, but that
the other girls' mothers never challenged her
presence. She said that she was amazed to see
the mother lose her temper and start beating
the shit out of her daughter!*
    Youth Center Intake Worker, New York City

In certain cases, the parents may be hostile yet have ambivalent feelings about acting out against their children's friends. This often happens when the parents believe or fear that their own children may leave home if they decide to make an issue of "harboring a fugitive." Rather than do something, they do nothing, and hope that the intrusion will pass quickly. However, doing nothing sometimes conjures up more than implied and results in a regular, but subtle, harrassment of the outsider. One youth who reported spending several weeks with a friend described this kind of harrassment:

*No one really said anything and that was the
problem. I started to feel like a piece of shit.
I mean people were a pain in the ass, without
even trying to be. They just sort of told you
they didn't want you there without having to
say so.*
                        Respondent number 7

A third type of parent is welfare focused and feels an obligation to provide food or shelter to children, despite the fact that a child's absence from home is illegitimate. In this circumstance, the parent does not approve of the absence but feels compelled to help on behalf of the child's welfare. Rather than turn the child back toward his home or toward an adverse street situation, the parent allows the child to remain in his home. In this circumstance, little trouble is experienced by the outsider and the arrangement continues until the young person chooses to leave. In these cases, the parents are often known to each other or the problems of

74

the family are known. Consequently, the parent is more tolerant of the situation.

As can be seen from the above, the use of friends to provide shelter can be a tricky business. How favorable such an experience proves to be often depends upon parent's position and the friend's ability to perceive how his parents are going to react.

Living Arrangements and Problems

Parents of friends, however, are not the only source of trouble for people on the run. Sometimes friends themselves become obstacles, threats and manipulators. This is especially true in the girlfriend—boyfriend arrangements, where the runner is emotionally and physically attached to the friend. Many times young people reported that such arrangements began alright but later became sources of conflict, challenge or manipulation. Much of this conflict is exemplified in the statement below:

> *At first, I really get along real nice with Larry, you know it just me and him, no problem. Then I got to see some of the stuff he was into, that I used to think was funny. Like dealing some dope. He used to deal a lot of goofballs, ya know, seconals and shit. Sometimes regular skag. People used to kid him about selling, some beat shit sometimes, but Larry would tell them to go deal somewhere else. Once I started living with him, I saw that he did used to beat the shit, mixing it with baking soda and stuff. I started to say that the people were right, he was selling beat shit. He told me to mind my business or get out so I left. I came back about a week later and we made up. Then, one afternoon we were over by the stores picking up some food and stuff and a whole bunch of motherfuckers just grabbed Larry and kicked his ass, just kicked his ass! They didn't touch me. The cops came, he went to the hospital. I went too, but right after that I cut out.*

> *Respondent number 16*

75

Many times problems with friends occur around the theme of sharing things or responsibilities.

> *I was living with this dude and he was expecting me to give him some money for rent. We had been friends for a long time before I left my home. Anyway, I tell him he's going to get his money as soon as I get work. I go down looking for a job but nothing seems to break for me. Finally, he tells me that his landlord wants to raise his rent because he has got me staying with him. He says he's got to have more money now! I tell him that I'll get it soon. When he hears this, he gets pissed off and shoves me out. I tell him to kiss my ass and leave.*
>
> *Respondent number 26*

Finally, several young people told me that situations with friends became bad because friends were no longer willing to help, be inconvenienced, or lie to parents. One respondent told me of an instance where he lived at a friend's house for about a month and then left in order to go live back in Washington, D.C. When the D.C. trip fell though, he naturally wanted to return to his old shelter. However, when he did return, his friend refused to help.

In other instances, respondents reported that their friends grew tired of making sacrifices, sharing and caring for someone other than themselves. Many of the breakdowns between runaways and friends need to be understood beyond one-to-one relationships or parent conflicts, to include the ever increasing demands that people away from home make. As was suggested by one respondent, who in the past helped others, of his own present predicament:

> *After a time you begin to get real confused. You finally get out of your house and things get better. Then you start to think about your future. You get in a bad mood and you start acting funny around people. Nobody wants yo you around them after awhile. You begin to put people in a bad head. You don't get any*

good messages from people; you know what I mean? I mean who wants somebody around who is a drag. You usually find out people got their own problems, so they don't need yours.

Respondent number 29

Such a situation typifies the events leading up to a breakdown between friends and eventual shift in residence and means of support.

Family

Very few respondents use family as a central means of support. Only eight respondents (22.2% of the sample) reported living with extended family members prior to contacting friends. This was especially true of white respondents, who reported using brother, sister, aunt, uncle or grandparent type contacts more than three times more often than did Black and Puerto Rican respondents.

As in the case of using friends, using family members for support includes a set of positive and negative features. First, on the negative side, the use of family requires more calculation and thought than does the use of friends.

All respondents suggested that family members very often receive advance notice of absence, and this can become a problem, especially if this information is fed from a parent's point of view, and on behalf of making certain you return home. Much like parents, older siblings and relatives feel compelled to honor family ties. Often, the implication of this is a return home, despite pleas for another course of action. In order to avoid this type of outcome, a person must calculate how understanding or "anti-parent" another relative will be. That is, will they help the situation; that is, "be cool," as many youth described it, or will they feel responsible; thus pursue and drag you home?

The second problem is that very often relatives' homes are too close to the child's own home. Being uncertain about where they wanted to be, many young people reported that "at first" they did, indeed, want to be where their parents might look!

The third problem, and somewhat allied to the second, is that although brothers, sisters and relatives may be sympathetic and far enough away from parents, they have already "had enough" of past family problems. Many respondents indicated that older family members left the house or were kicked out for the same reasons as they were and were tired of getting involved or getting into arguments over recurrent family matters. One respondent said that his mother warned his older sister that if "she let him stay with her, she was going to have both their asses locked up."

Such parent-child conflicts don't appear unusual, as evidenced by the following description of an earlier family court battle between a set of family members having different perceptions of what the problem was:

> We had just left court; it was me, mom and my two sisters. My mother was still arguing with me and telling me she didn't know what I wanted. She was warning me about school and telling me that if I didn't stay home, we would be back in court. She said she never had such problems with the others (sisters). Right then, my sister told her to stop fucking yelling and this set the four of us off! My sister was crying and telling my mother that she was just making things worse with the yelling. She said that things wouldn't get no better if she kept forcing me to do things. She told my mother she was crazy, that things were different today. I know my mother didn't agree, she just didn't say anything to my sister, nothing. We all stopped talking when we got on the bus. After that, my mother and her just didn't speak much after that.
>
> Respondent number 16

On the positive side, the use of families offers a certain protection from being manipulated and eases the transition period after leaving home. When I explored this dimension with respondents, all reported having a trust in family members that they did not have for friends. Many people described this trust as different for friends as compared with family — as something that family members do for you because they know you. For example, one person reported that he did not have to be "hip" or "rough" around his brothers. He said his brothers had been with him a long time and they "knew what he was about," — with friends this was not the case. Most respondents said that they had to be on guard even after they were being helped. A role performance (Goffman, 1961) was the theme here and when among family members, such a performance was not necessary.

Unfortunately, not all could depend on family members. Respondents were often the oldest child and for them there were no sibling resources. Others reported no other family contact in the area, while some suggested they did not know how to reach family members. These type of respondents tended to seek out friends first, since family contacts were not really in the realm of possibility. Regarding family resources, it should be pointed out that some young people appeared to know more, have more contacts with, understand, and respect other family members. For such youth, seeking the help of family was the preferred choice over friends. However, it would be incorrect to conceive of this issue as an either/or circumstance, since both resources are used in some cases as a compliment to each other. Such a circumstance was neatly portrayed during one interview during which resources were explored:

> *You see when I need cash, I can always go to my brother or his wife. I try to pay them back but I know they will give it to me anyway. So long as I don't go up there everyday. Course I knew he would rather give me some cash than have me live with them. He figures that a little bit of money will help out and it does. He comes up with a little cash and I don't ask to stay over. Now I got some money and a place to stay since I know I can stay with my friends anyway.*
>
> *Respondent number 16*

Another case in which this combination helps is when an unusual circumstance comes up, as for instance when arrest or violence is a real possibility.

> *I figured that once they kicked his ass like*

79

> *that, that was enough for me! So I right away*
> *called my sister and told her I wanted to talk*
> *to her. She was glad to hear from me and told*
> *me to come right over. I did and that's where*
> *I am staying now. It's working out okay and*
> *plus that I can find out what has been happen-*
> *ing in my house with the court and shit.*
>
> *Respondent number 22*

Relatives offer an almost natural refuge for young people. Thus, it is of little surprise that many youth choose not to fall back on family on a regular basis, but only in extreme circumstances.

One final point about relying on families as refuge pertains to its episodic nature. Most young people I spoke with only relied upon family-related support when it was necessary. For the eight youths who reported initial uses of family upon leaving home, most young people relied on family only in "problem episodes." One young person, for example, reported that upon running away from a court-ordered group resident, he went directly to his brother and sister-in-law. He reported:

> *I didn't know what else to do. I figured that if*
> *I went home my mother would only call the*
> *cops and that would be that.*
>
> *Respondent number 21*

This and similar serious episodes serve as the background upon which the family gets called into action. How frequently such contacts occur, then, becomes very dependent upon what problem episodes unfold for the young person.

Runaway Programs

A third source of shelter and welfare is the runaway program. Although only two respondents reported an initial use of such facilities, all knew about their operation and all but one respondent had periodic contact with them. Within New York City, there exists several different types of runaway services, each with distinct ideology and features. The use of such services often occurs after a young person has

80

either run out of understanding friends and relatives, is in between having left family and friends, and is finding a replacement, or has been referred through a court or welfare agency. Responses concerning the use of runaway facilities indicate that older youth (sixteen to twenty) are more in need of the use of such services than are younger persons. Moreover, services are viewed as more helpful to older persons than younger ones. The table below summarizes responses made to the issue of how often runaway services are used by age.

TABLE 9

THE USE OF PROGRAM SERVICES BY AGE

	10 - 15	16 - 20
Has used service	40%	90%
	(10)	(10)
Has not used service	60%	10%
	(15)	(1)
	100%	100%
	(25)	(11)

Similar to the resources of family and friends, runaway programs offer advantages and disadvantages. An advantage of most runaway programs is that they offer an immediate solution to the problem of finding refuge. Such programs are funded for the purpose of assisting youth away from home, and young people understand this. Going to such a program offers a quick way out of a difficult situation. A second advantage is that help can be obtained from people who are not going to confront them regarding absence. A young person need not immediately acknowledge his problems with friends or family; this can come later. At first they are only counting on the services of a program and thus avoid the embarrassment of having to beg help in exchange for having to adhere to beliefs of the program. This is especially important when a young person finds him or herself without residence because of having to leave the home of family or friends. A third advantage is that, beyond residence, many programs offer medical services, counseling, and leads on employment, education and similar services. These sort of services are especially im-

81

portant to older youth who find it increasingly important to plan out and develop marketable skills in order to alter their present circumstances. As observed by one young man:

> *I figured that if I get some training in a couple of things, I'll be okay. I went down to talk to a guy the other day about a job. He wanted to know if I ever had any training on working with cars. I told him no but said that I did a lot of work in D.C. He told me that was real good but that one time he hired a guy with that kind of experience. He told me that this just didn't work out. The guy didn't have enough background and that he was too slow. I kinda felt he would have given me the job had I said I was getting some training.*
> *Respondent number 29*

However, receiving training, medical attention, or counseling does not come without some type of trade-off, as evidenced by the following comment:

> *You see you can go in then at first and rap and get help and shit, but the people expect you to take a good look at yourself. I mean at first you can bullshit, but later on you gonna have to let the program people see that you are trying to help yourself. You need to play by the rules, keep or find some work, not bullshit around. You can't go running around all night, there are house rules that you need to obey if you want to stay around and be helped.*
> *Respondent number 29*

But runaway programs do require an adherence to rules since there are other residents and their welfare to consider. This might be viewed as one disadvantage in dealing with programs. Programs, by definition, provide structure and routine. In many cases, this is the very sort of structure respondents objected to in connection with leaving home. Thus, the young person is once again confronted with certain demands and expectations—which somewhat like the home setting, require some level oi compliance. In some cases, this presents a problem to certain young people and they simply run away again.

A second disadvantage in dealing with programs is that it is difficult to manipulate the program to an individual's personal advantage. A young person cannot simply go there and do anything he or she wishes   controls do exist. In addition, program staff either fully understand runaway problems or are former runaways themselves. Consequently, it is difficult to confuse, manipulate, or falsely present yourself. Unlike friends or family, program personnel challenge or probe your reasons for leaving or your plans to return home since they, as a program, intensively need to justify their existence.

Runaway Concerns, Events and Activities

There are three typical events or activities which make up a day in the life of a runaway. Discussion of these events or activities follow under the headings of employment, education, "hanging out" and hustling.

Each of these headings covers a wide range of activities and a good deal of variability exists among styles of working, hanging out or hustling. No one spends his entire day at only one activity, but rather at several different types, all in an effort to secure a regular lifestyle.

Employment and Education

Three out of every four respondents interviewed reported that they were no longer in school. This figure is even higher for Black respondents, since only one person of the total Black respondents' group reported himself as still enrolled in school. Respondents over the age of sixteen, for the most part, dismissed the idea of school enrollment. They tended to have been away from school the longest and very often did not see school as worthy of discussion. They most often discussed the need for alternatives to school, such as training in occupation programs or remedial services.

Although the majority of respondents reported no longer being in school, this was not always a clear-cut decision in the minds of some young people. When I questioned young people on whether they could return to school if they so desired, or if they were actually dismissed from school, only a few respondents knew. Students assume that they have been dismissed from school for absence, even when they are as young as thirteen or fourteen. This view of no longer being eligible for school was summarized by one program representative in the following quote:

> *These kids usually have one bad problem after another in school. Marks, discipline, attendance, etc. Many of their friends also have problems and they support each other. Pretty soon it makes little sense for them to go, so they don't. Day after day is spent around the school, but none actually attends. Sometimes parents become involved at this point, the school informs them of problems. Most often this does little good since the parent's reaction is hostile and both the kid and the school back off. Eventually, the school begins to ignore the kid and after a point, the kid feels he doesn't have to attend. No one tells them not to attend! They simply stop showing up.*
> *Youth Worker, New York City*

The culmination of this process is the abandonment of school and the beginning in search of other activities. Very often this search gets interrupted by a need for finding employment.

Regardless of age, every respondent expressed an interest in having a job. Much like education, older respondents find it more "essential" to have a job than do younger respondents. When this issue was explored further, most respondents equated having a job with having money, and with money they reported being able to go places and do things. Many young people view being out of school as an opportunity to seek a job. Up until this time, school hours, school days and homework interfered with the job search. Few people attributed age or lack of experience to their reason for not working. Approximately 80% of all respondents suggested that they had attempted to look for work prior to leaving their homes. In many instances, the need to work versus the need to go to school represented a source of conflict in the homes. Youth reported having to spend a good deal of time explaining this issue to parents. In some cases, this was the principal reason for leaving home.

Unfortunately, the search for work appears no easier out of the home than it is within it. The opportunities to find work are scarce, and they are often based on who you know since few respondents had much in the way of marketable skills. Moreover, few could legally hold fulltime jobs. As one respondent put it:

> *You might get some kinda jive-ass job (hit-or-miss) but nobody is gonna give a kid any everyday job.*
>
> *Respondent number 21*

Of all the respondents spoken to, a total of six people reported having part-time work. During this investigation, six respondents were spoken with continuously over the course of a six month period. Not one was able to obtain fulltime employment in New York City. In this period, two persons were able to get one shot, shape-up work, but this was on a part-time basis and it paid very little. Throughout the interviews with young respondents, this talk was always brought up. Many viewed the inability to find work as a crisis because they did not understand why it was so difficult to do. Some expected themselves to be much more capable and in demand than they actually were, while others offered no opinion.

When describing the employment needs, aspirations or concerns of young people out of their home, it is important that we consider several dimensions which were reported to reinforce the theme of looking for work. These include:
    (a)   the status of young workers,
    (b)   the theme of work as a vehicle for independence, and
    (c)   work as an alternative to hanging out or hustling.
Each of these were unifying concepts within our conversations.

With Respect To Experience

All of the respondents were young, inexperienced and eager to work. All lacked training and few had any firm idea about the type of work they wished to do. An employer could see runaways as a cheap source of labor; however, this was not the case. One reason for this is that they lack a work discipline. Most respondents reported having problems with the expectations of the work world; namely, with the issue of time and attendance. Also, wages were a problem, and much lower than many young people expected. Consequently, among runaways there is little determination to stick to a job. Turnover becomes the norm — if someone is lucky enough to get a job.

Work and Independence

Many respondents equated work with acquiring and maintaining independence. But not all respondents viewed work as the only means to gain independence. Some spoke of physical abilities, toughness, etc.; others of being out of their home and doing what they wanted as independence. However, for those who viewed independence as something that lets one do what one wants in a problem or crisis, then work was a source of independence. Each of the people I spoke with acknowledged that work brought money and money allows choice. Young persons in this investigation understood this clearly. Not all made this observation in a flat statement but all, during our discussions, pointed out the sort of problems one can avoid with money, such as the rules and regulations one must adhere to in a runaway program, or the pointless waiting by a phone all day for a call concerning a job lead.

Below is a short excerpt of a conversation conducted with an eighteen-year-old male concerning the lack of money, choices and independence.

Q: So I would take it then that you feel this program offers help?
A: Yes, but you got to understand I didn't need this! (with emphasis)
Q: Could you explain this to me more?
A: You see, if I had my choice I would have my ass in the street but there is nothing there now. I had a job at the Bingo Hall in Jamaica part time last month. This gave me money and I could go fuck around, you know hang out, I could do things. Now, I ain't got that, the guy said I couldn't work there no more. So you see I ain't got no money, no job and I got to be here.

Q: Well, what about your friends?

A: Friends, shit, some of them are here themselves. You can only stay in the street so long without money; you got to go running around and steal or get a bag (pocketbook). Then you get busted.

Q: Has that happened to you?

A: Shit, yeah, what do you think I'm here for. If you've done stealing, then you know what that is like. Cops get you, they bust your ass. They know you. It ain't worth it.

Q: So I take it you wish to leave.

A: Yea, when I get a job, I'll get a crib (apartment) and do what I want.

A final point regarding independence is that the understanding that independence and choice usually goes beyond the mere matters of fun and freedom. Although young persons, like anyone else, value their freedom and the good life, they recognize that becoming independent offers more than that. Speaking with respondents over the course of several weeks, it became clear that they were aware of societal pressures to be your "own man" and be independent. Each recognized that people expect you to be independent and alert and think of you as funny if you don't have clear ideas and feelings about life. Each recognized that as long as you are successful, people will like you. Many instances were described by young people involved in legal, as well as illegal activities, and in each instance a successful outcome was viewed as the most important concern of all parties involved. Young persons could reach such an outcome only if they were independent and strong people who know "what is happening," in the words of one respondent. This position was especially true of the two respondents who had spent time in state training schools and who, upon returning to their old hangouts, noticed the need to "grow up and be their own man." One noted:

People don't wanna hear that shit about you being young and that stuff. You are not young. . .your big. People ain't gonna play around no more. They will tell you, 'you ain't no little kid, I'll kick your ass if you give me any trouble'.

Similarly, in terms of work, the need to become more self-sufficient becomes more critical the older you get:

> *When I returned home from training school, I think everybody figured I was okay. You know, a good school record, get a job, things like that. Well I gets to talk with mom and she says look, I can't keep you and give you money everyday for you to play with. She said that I was too old to play, that I have to get a job, help her out around the house. She says that it's only her money we got to live on. I told her that I was 'down' for a job and that I was looking for one but I had to do other things, too. She said I didn't have to do nothing but work, as far as she could see, and that I better get some work fast! You see, I figured that some work, some school, you know, like that. Now, I got to look for some bullshit job with no school. Shit, you know what kind of job you get with that!*

Respondent number 29

Thus, beyond the concern for fun or friends, work allows a young person to announce themselves and become more like the person adults around them feel they should be — a responsible, strong and successful person.

Work As An Alternative To Hustling and Hanging Out

A commonplace feeling among young people away from home is that if you aren't working, you need either to hustle or hang out. Like all other social settings, being away from home demands that certain activities be engaged in to fill the day. Since such a large number of my respondents were without work, much of the interim discussion focused on what somebody does when he doesn't have a job. Respondents talked about hustling or hanging out as the alternative and did so in a manner different from talking about looking for work.

When speaking about the issue of looking for a job, many were reserved in speech and clearcut as to what sort of job they wished to have. Most saw the importance of work and the end results and some respondents felt such end results were worth pursuing. That was not the case with the descriptions and discussions regarding hustling and hanging out. Both these activities, which will be described in further detail below, were spoken about with a sense of confusion. Most persons reported that hanging out was "bullshit" after you did it for a long time, because it was the same old thing — a routine. Many reported and described encounters with police while hanging out. Hanging out in the course of the day was done to kill time, because there was little to do, or because you were waiting to get a job or go speak to someone about a job. Hanging out, as a term, included a variety of behaviors which ranged from loitering off a stoop or in a park during the summer, to going to a dance hall-disco in the early hours of morning. In general, it was something young people did when they had nothing else to do—a source of fun at one point, boredom at another. Many respondents talked about doing nothing and hanging out immediately after leaving home, but growing tired of the routine after awhile. No respondents seemed very clearcut on what the end results of hanging out were—except for a possible encounter with the police or the ability to kill time. However, when speaking about hanging out, most young people described it as something that could lead to hustling.

"Hustling" is an act which is understood to be illegal and is engaged in for gain. As indicated below, at least 40% of my sample engaged in some form of hustling. Here again, however, respondents were not clear, in many cases, about when some act constituted a hustle, or what someone gets in return for the hustle, or when someone becomes committed to a hustle. Interpreting these descriptions of hustling and hanging out, the following quote best sums up the feeling of many that work is preferable:

> *After a while, you can just sit around with your friends so long. I mean hanging out is okay and all, but shit you can't get over by sitting there. I need a job more than I need to sit around. If I don't get one pretty soon, I'm*

gonna have to get into the hustle, what else can
I do?

Hustling

Forty percent of all respondents reported that they had engaged in some work of hustling since they had left home. Of the 40%, the majority of respondents reporting such behavior were male and fifteen or sixteen years of age.

Hustling can be described as the systematic procedure used by an actor to take something of value, material or emotional, from another actor. Hustling is performed in a number of settings, for various reasons, and with various degrees of participant recognition of being hustled. Furthermore, the hustling act appears to have very few requirements – little technical skill is needed.

It has been keenly point out by Irwin (1970) that: "Although hustlers borrow some of the traits of the confidence man, they do not have the technical skill for the big con" (p. 13). This observation is very descriptive of the hustling activities reported by young people away from home; for the most part, they were small, insignificant and based upon need. As in the case of the labor market, most youth brought the disabilities of being young, inexperienced and in need of instant gratification. Only two youths reported an immediate ability (at the time of our interview) to hook up with the "man," and get into a hustle "if necessary, as being part of the team."

In general, there are two ways to hustle. One uses the body and the other the mind. The "mind" hustles are similar to the flim-flam and gambling men types, who are glorified in the deep south.[7] However, their level of sophistication and practice is small or almost non-existent, when compared to the sharp-talking, flim-flam man or gambler. Some examples of hustles engaged in by young people include piss water cologne, the pocketbook hustle, fireworks hustle, beating the subway, the job hustle, and working as a team with their man in card games (i.e., three card monte or twenty-one), where the action is quick and the profit fast.[8]

The cologne hustle is the selling of soapy water, instead of cologne to an unsuspecting street corner consumer. This is especially popular on a holiday when people purchase more and where the salesmen can keep moving around. The pocketbook hustle is accomplished by starting a fight or flareup on a street corner, subway stop, etc., and while the victim is involved in the confusion in the street, grabbing the handbag and running, to meet later in an agreed upon place. Sometimes bags are grabbed without staging a scene but that depends upon how much experience the person has at bag snatching to begin with. The fireworks hustle is similar to dope hustles described by drug addicts in recalling their own means of support while on the street (Palenski, 1972), p. 60), except that both the hustler and victim are younger. Here the object is for one young man to approach a group of boys who want to buy fireworks. A sample fireworks is displayed for the interested buyer; with excitement the boys pool their money and one youth accompanies the salesman in order to pick up the fireworks. Upon arrival, the young man is accosted for the money and obviously becomes a victim of robbery.

Three main themes are important to persons discussing the mind hustle and they tended to surface in conversations with runaways, again and again. The first theme is that many persons were victims themselves before they decided to go out hustling. For example, in the job hustles, two people split the "employment agency fee," while one gets the job. One young man told me the purpose here is to eventually split the salary earned on the job and be able to afford another fee and thus, another job. This person was lured into this scheme and did not get a job or money and never saw his alleged friend again.

The second theme is practice. The more you practice, the better you become and the more contact you are apt to have with other people engaged in hustling. Also, the more experience you have with hustling, the more able you are to estimate the return and risk you will get on a certain brand of hustle. For example, one person reported not wanting to get into a card game hustle because you had to work the Garden (Madison Square Garden) and there are usually too many cops and consequently too much of a risk. He reported that other hustles are easier and more money is made. Also, several persons reported that if many hustlers work in a neighborhood, etc., it is a lot easier than if a hustler is working alone, as it was described by one respondent:

91

I'm not saying that the whole thing is hustling but shit, I heard guys talk at school (Training School) and I can do a lot better than them. They talked a lot of punk shit, none of them can get over. Now I know I can get over, cause my brothers is hustlers, they can hustle, they can take it when they have to and I have seen them do it. It's easy.

Respondent number 10

A third theme is not getting "locked up." Staying out of jail represents the difference between being a hustler and being a thief. In certain cases, a very thin line exists between actual theft and the hustle. Many youth expressed the opinion that you ain't taking nothing when you hustle, yet all were afraid of police. The act of taking is more subtle in the hustle than in outward theft. However, much depends on the type of hustle being discussed. For instance, hustles can be viewed in a hierarchy from the simplest ones, such as jumping turnstiles, to the more obnoxious ones, such as beating up a kid who has been set up to purchase fireworks. Most youth were not as threatened by the mind hustle and being involved in it as they were in the body or sex hustle, which is the other type that can be engaged in.

Body Hustle

According to the Director of the Port Authority Police Runaway Unit, sex is a market which is always looking for buyers and sellers. To people on the street, the sex market provides to some degree a way to hustle with your body.

In my conversations with respondents, there was not one person identified who engaged in "regular hired-hand sex" as a means of survival. But a pattern of loose, yet structured ways, of using the body in exchange for cash was discussed. Apparently, this system often evolves out of contacts and friends that a young person makes while away from home and that this system minimizes coercion and force.

For example, one young woman who was a regular at one of the most popular runaway projects was alleged to be living with a pimp on the West Side in a well-to-do apartment. When questioned, this person replied that this man befriended her several months back, and invited her to stay at his place (in a separate room) if she needed to until such time as she was ready to go it alone. She indicated that although she thought that this man was a pimp, he never bothered her (she was fifteen). There was no force or violence issues in her discussion.

The question of whether she is obliged to engage in sex while at the apartment in exchange for room and board can be asked. Her presentation of friendship rather than abuse when speaking of the setup also offered a clear idea that she could do what she wanted to, where she wished to. However, considering the possibility of a false presentation on her part, there are other criteria which might help estimate or better interpret her story.

Dorothy Bracey (1977), in a recent study of juvenile prostitution in New York City, suggested that underage prostitution can cause considerable problems for pimps (p. 22). Being underage can maximize police contact and pimps normally wish to minimize such contact. Thus, it is best for the pimp not to get involved with an underage person. Also, young kids can cause problems simply because they often cannot be predicted or trusted (Bracey). Thus, it may not be in a pimp's interest to get involved in certain cases.

In this instance, however, another respondent close to this woman said that, indeed, she was not being a prostitute for money but that sooner or later she would, probably when she got a little older or a little closer so that she could trust him. Such an arrangement depicts the no-strings-attached, but regular routine of a sex business.

Another example of such a routine follows: It is taken from an actual encounter and described by a young male who frequents the apartment of an "old guy" whom he "stays around with" and who wants sex:

> *Once in a while I go over to my friends apartment and there will be these guys there. You don't have to do nothin but like hang out, it's a party. After the party, the guy usually asks me if I need to stay over, he knows I was in a bad way because he sees me at the bingo hall and knows I need a good job. Anyway, he asks me if I want to stay at his place and I say NO!*

Now when I go back there, I take my friend.
My friend says he wants to stay with him, he
thinks I should also.

Respondent number 3

A third example is taken from a young person explaining her encounters with her boyfriend and his business.

I was living with this guy, you see we liked
each other and he wasn't too old. Well, we
would get it on and everything was real good.
One time, he says I got to help his 'club,' and
that I need to be there on Friday nights. I said
okay, but when I went there, people start
grabbing your body, they are high and shit, so
everybody thinks its fun but you, shit, I
ain't living there no more and I'm glad, it ain't
worth the hassle. If he thinks I'm going to be
into that kind of business. . .no way!

Respondent number 33

Once again, each of these statements emphasizes that an unacceptable pattern is identified (at least in part) by young people,[9] yet their requirements and demands to belong are somewhat variable.

Program workers attributed these patterns to the age of my sample (younger) and the narrow focus of my exploration on sex. Several workers pointed out that young persons are used to recruit friends into a sex enterprise (or are used in sex movies) and sometimes serve as informants. Indeed, if the discussion on sex market activity were broadened to include such activities, then probably a more coercive, violent or mandatory picture would have emerged. However, this investigation did not attempt to intensively explore sex activity but only to link it as a means of survival and hustle to the type mentioned above. In doing so, sexual exploitation, as a means of exchange, was reported as minimal by respondents.

During this investigation, young people indicated the mind hustles were much preferred to hustling with the body, for the reasons noted above. However, anyone who had used one was aware of the other. That is, young people generally drift (Matza, 1971) to "where the action is," they "stay

94

loose" and there are routines of response if problems develop. Since, in addition to hustling, young people reported friends, programs, relations, etc., as solutions, perhaps people choose not to have sex for money. Perhaps they choose not to get involved in what they consider the "worst of all possibilities" unless there is a dramatic reduction of alternative avenues of survival; e.g., contacts, residence, use of programs and the ability to hustle in other ways. However, this type of development is least likely to occur, especially if a runaway has been developing acceptable resources all the while. Many young people interviewed in this sample considered selling one's self for money the least preferred route to travel — especially when others can be chosen instead.

Hanging Out

"Hanging out," is an expression commonly used among youth to represent a wide range of non-work, non-hustle behavior. To hang out is to relax and to momentarily suspend the more concrete concerns of the day. Such behavior can occur anywhere, be engaged in by anyone and take up varying degrees of a person's day. Hanging out is usually done in settings where full actor involvement or attention to detail is required; such as, parks, street corners. Behavior in such settings is very diffuse and no one is expected to perform any predefined task or mutual obligation. In short, to hang out is to engage in free movement and spontaneous relaxation. A wide range of behavior falls into this category.

The experiences while hanging out, reported by young people, varied from idling, riding through New York City trains for fun, to spending someone else's money in a night spot (disco), or simply loitering in the Times Square area. All youth spoken with reported that much of their day is spent hanging out and doing nothing in particular. During this investigation, much of that activity characterized as hanging out resembled a type of "group loitering." Moreover, it typically was boring — with the degree of boredom varying from situation to situation.

There was nothing special in the activity spoken about here. In most aspects it resembled any other "killing time activity" engaged in by any youth generation. However, the significance of the "hanging out" activity is not in the act but rather in its ability to serve as a social base where young people meet each other and as a substitute for work or hustling. Based upon interviews and observations in the field, both these issues are important to the person away from home – especially when he has no particular or consistent place of residence or means of support.

Meeting Other People

Because hanging out behavior occurs in a casual atmosphere, the rules, level of involvement, etc., that actors feel compelled to bring to such a setting is minimal. Young people freely come and go in hangout situations – few ties exist and the emphasis is clearly on fun, enjoyment, excitement and exchanges. Given this set of circumstances, most young persons approach the situation with the idea of capitalizing on it. Most persons referred to or described the act of hanging out as going to see "what was happening," moving around or seeing what others are doing.

Just where a person decided to hang out depended upon whether or not he or she has a job, money or living accommodations. The few respondents who held jobs reproted very little time spent hanging out. It was made clear during conversations that holding down a job takes up a good portion of the day. There is little time to explore or to relax. Respondents reported that those having safe and secure living arrangements with friends engaged in hanging out more often than those living with relatives, relying on programs or in temporary search of residence. One implication of these patterns is that people sharing the hospitality of friends feel more compelled to engage in the activities their friends engage in. Staying in someone's home somewhat compels you to follow along with the crowd. In general, respondents who were working, or were living with friends felt less compelled to use hangout as a vehicle for bettering one's situation. This is illustrated in the following statement made by one male:

> *You see things are okay for now. No problems, no cops and no hassles. I can go out, do what I want. I don't have to worry about not going home shit and no begging for a place to stay. I don't have to sniff around or kiss nobody's ass.*
> *Respondent number 17*

When I questioned, "Would things be different if you weren't in such good shape?", the following response was given:

> *You bet, last time I was out, I didn't know what to do. It was difficult for me to hook up with people because I didn't know who would be down with me and help me. I spent half the day worrying about where I could stay and what I could eat. I don't have that problem now, I can go where I want and do what I want; hang out, party, have a good time.*
> *Respondent number 17*

Unfortunately, many respondents weren't in such a good situation and they devoted much of their time to seeking out new work contacts, survival leads, etc., while they were hanging out. For example, during my observations in one West Side nightspot, a young man, who for most of the evening was having fun, abruptly switched his interest to the topic of employment when it was overheard that the club was looking for a daytime clean-up man. As I began to observe his interest in the job, we talked about the problem of working and the importance of this possible job. Based upon this conversation, it became very clear that runaways need to "hook into a job" wherever they can. Another example is when a young person canvasses an area for a job with friends while they are simultaneously taking in the sites, harrassing shoppers or just watching people. In these circumstances, young people might capture a quick job, use it as a means of support briefly and meet new people. Job opportunities such as "sidewalk guards" for cheap drygoods stores or piecework janitors[10] are typical, since they are in locations where hanging out usually takes place.

Beyond work, hanging around provides a social basis for hearing and sharing information. For example, one young person received an education in runaway programs because he was present in the hanging out location.

The type of concern and ultimate reaction from police dealing with runaways versus non-police agencies is somewhat different. Police are more prone to force specific choices onto youth and this type of attitude is frowned upon by young people. But sharing information on such topics of mutual concern increases one's understanding of where a young person can seek help.

There are unique temporal considerations for young people out of their homes. For example, although we conventionally think about our clock as being broken up into a twenty-four hour day, with a morning, afternoon, early evening, etc., young people often perceive time differently, and in terms of certain events, opportunities, or responsibilities. For example, a youth might indicate "you need to get to welfare early" for emergency relief or residence, or warn a peer "don't get caught short" in residence on a Friday because weekend placement is poor or almost non-existent. After 2:00 a.m., many of the people found in nightspots, fast food shops, riding trains, etc., begin to drop their guards and it becomes easier to do things like steal, hustle or loiter. Finally, special temporal concerns are devoted to the people who work the off-hours—the police, the all-night coffee shops and fast food shops, free breakfast haunts, sympathetic crash pads, etc., Queens General and Bellevue Hospital. In a "hit or miss" lifestyle, such general information can become a part-time preoccupation.

This was evidenced in an informal discussion among myself and two young people regarding police:

> *1st Commentator: You know its pretty important to know what the cops will let you do.*
>
> *My response: Why so?*
>
> *1st Commentator: Well, like this way you know where you can hang out and where you can't. Cops don't always fuck with you in all places, sometimes they say "later."*
>
> *My response: Well, like can you give me an example.*
>
> *2nd Respondent: Sure, like in front of the clubs, nobody will say shit to you then, there nobody is interested, too much happening! It's like nobody cares.*
>
> *1st Respondent: Yea, like also by Nathan's,*

like you can go over there and unless the
cops are told to bother you, they won't.
My response: So then you are saying that some
places are better to be in than others?
Both Respondents: Yep, and I'm gonna be in
a safe place.
Respondents number 27 and 28

Some of the information that youth exchange or contacts they make only concern immediate problems. Conversations consist of war stories, macho stories, or updates on
personal court cases and detention settings. Often these
express concerns when someone is taken off the street
by police via an arrest or a warrant. Youth reported that you
can get a "pretty good idea about what is happening at
court" or what can happen to you, when you speak to
people.

I met this one dude at Spofford and he ran
down all shit that can happen to you. It turns
out that you eventually get cut loose (go
home). The court can't hold you and if it does,
you beg your mother and she can talk to the
court for you. Sometimes the court will send
you to some kinda home, and that sort of
place is easy to split from.

Such conversations, over time, make young people
well equipped at making estimates and decisions concerning
jail, parents, courts, etc. This theme is well-supported by a
member of program personnel who reported "indeed, many
young people appear on the scene understanding the 'game'
and, as soon as they can, they can apply their gamesmenship
to cutting out or making the situation better for themselves." Thus, by the time young people cross paths with
institutional settings, they have already estimated, through
friends, "what the stakes are."

Substitute For Work And Hustling
When a young person isn't working or engaged in some
sort of hustle, a good part of the day goes unfulfilled. In such

cases, the hanging out act serves as a filler of time. Most youth reported that "when you don't have a job, you hang out a lot." On first impression, and through my own brief experiences, such activity seemed pointless and boring. However, such impressions quickly faded as I recognized the character of such behavior, or the moment-to-moment significance of the action. Much of the action takes place for fun.

During the course of my observation and analysis, fun surfaced as one reason people hang out. Based upon my own reflections, to proceed along such a course is of value and, in the absence of anything else, such enjoyment becomes important. Enjoyment can range from the casual jostling on trains, to the deliberate annoyance of passengers, to the casual glancing of passersby as someone tries to half-heartedly panhandle money. Youth reported that they often do a lot of the same things in the street that they did at home and that they often try to go back around where they live in order to find out if they can go home. Such behavior serves a definite purpose. It keeps them doing something and this is important to someone who is trying to make sense out of things. It also allows people to check out a home situation which they might want to return to at some future point. As one person put it:

> *What am I going to do? No job, and you try getting one. No way to make money. What else can you do but hang out? Sometimes you can hook up with something just by hanging out.*
> Respondent number 29

CHAPTER FOOTNOTES

[1] In this investigation the descriptive data may be looked upon as the "first level of material" gathered on the meaning worlds (i.e., their viewpoints) of my subjects.

[2] A complete discussion on sample selection, data gathering obstacles, etc., can be found in the earlier chapter on methods.

[3] *Perspective on Runaway Youth, A Special Report*, Ken Libertoff, Massachusetts Committee on Children and Youth, Boston, Massachusetts, 1976.

4Two examples of such studies are *Homeless Youth in New York City: A Field Study*, Theodore G. Hackman, and *A Summary Report on Youth Runaways*, New York City Youth Board, 1976.

5Special schools in this case were "alternative variety" schools, often run by the New York City Office of Probation and the Board of Education.

6This four year absence revolved around the young person being placed into a Division for Youth Facility where, upon his release, he found his family "moved away," and he stated that he has not been able to find them.

7Irwin (1970) has suggested that this set of practices has a very long and ordered history in this country. (See *The Felon*, Prentice Hall, 1970).

8For a recent description of this activity, see Earl Caldwell, *New York Daily News* article, August 7, 1979.

9I think it somewhat premature to speak of an actual structure in operation here but, rather, a set of patterns which vary in their intensity. That is, actual social boundaries do exist as they would exist for some other activity such as "going to school." Yet actors understand and recognize the routine set of expectations characteristic of such settings.

10Such typical jobs can be seen in and around the Chambers Street and 14th Street areas of Manhattan.

CHAPTER VI

BECOMING A RUNAWAY

In the previous chapter, I sketched the concerns and day-to-day activities which make up a runaway routine. To the extent that such a cluster of activities was described by respondents, one could acquire a basic understanding of what young people do while outside of home. However, to demonstrate how such activity contributes to a runaway identity, it is necessary to show how much activity gradually replaces the behavior engaged in while home.

From Conventional to Unconventional

This investigation views becoming a runaway as essentially a process of moving from a conventional, or in-home, to an unconventional, or out-of-home, lifestyle.[1] As Becker (1963) states, ". . .the onset of deviance suggests that individuals have come to abandon the rules, norms, etc. of a conventional setup in favor of a less acceptable, socially frowned upon or negative setup." Becker's position is simple:

> People do not become deviant because they have a stake in conventional society. Rather they have learned a set of roles, values, beliefs, concerns, etc., which are contrary to the anticipated roles, values, beliefs, concerns, etc., of society at large. Such a process can be contrasted with the behavior defined as 'normal' since the person no longer is viewed as being tied to a conventional lifestyle or pattern, they are different.

As the process of becoming deviant applies to runaways, a youth can be viewed as a "runner" only after he/she has given up some of the conventional in-the-home concerns and replaced them with the concerns dictated by an out-of-home lifestyle.

There is a gradual process in which someone slowly moves from the status of family member to former family member. Young people encounter everyday circumstances which ultimately transform home concerns, opinions, interests, justifications and familiar terrains to those of the runaway setting.

Listed below are steps which this study identifies as most often occurring en route to achieving a runaway status. Since individuals bring different backgrounds and skills to any situation, these steps do not always occur in the order presented below. However, each is important in the overall transformation of young people into runaways.

Deciding To Run Away

There are a number of different reasons why people choose to leave home. In some instances, several factors combine to make the situation totally unbearable and absence becomes the preferred choice. However, despite this range of reasons, few young persons simply decide to run away out of the blue.

This does not mean that people leave home without plans, but the decision to leave is usually gradual. Several different variables play important roles in this process. They include (1) family involvement or lack of involvement; (2) peer examples; (3) propitious situations; and (4) shrinking alternatives.

These factors do not only influence the decision to leave but also have additional importance because they make the home a less preferred choice. For example, most young persons reported the initial need and willingness to work out their home problems. However, in most cases, this proved futile and young people eventually felt that remaining home made little sense.

Family Involvement

Family involvement is a major factor influencing the process of deciding to run away from home. Family involvement may be defined as the amount of time young people devote, or are asked to devote, to other family members and matters. Most young people interviewed in this study reported that prior to leaving home, they felt their involvement in family affairs to be minimum. For some, the everyday routine of being a member, being interested, responsible or accountable to family was no longer important.

These feelings of not wanting to belong are best exemplified by the following statements:

> *Being home on time and being able to explain where you were was always on my mind. This always was something I would think about before I reached home. After awhile, I didn't see why I should have to explain. My friends didn't to their parents. I began to see a whole lot didn't make sense. I began to see the way my father acted toward me was wrong. I just decided to do something about it, like I said to myself, forget about him and worry about you. Soon I didn't have to think about him or his explanations anymore.*
>
> *Respondent number 33*

> *I found myself slowly being left out. If you can't talk to anybody, you're left out. They would ask me about school or about what I was planning to do about my not helping around the house. All those things weren't worth talking about. Every time we got together, we talked about my problems.*
>
> *Respondent number 36*

> *It was always not doing something that I would get ripped up for. After a while, I just listened and didn't say anything. I figured why bother.*
>
> *Respondent number 30*

> *I figured if we was going to court, there was nothing I could do to change things.*
>
> *Respondent number 30*

As pointed out by respondents, such encounters, when isolated, presented little problem. However, once they became regular, home life became uncomfortable. Most young people reaching this point in their family life did not report a need for altering the home situation. However, as their contact and family involvement became less frequent, the other influences began to become attractive and relied on.

While the young person is still in the home, this can further place a distance between the individual and family members, since many young people reported the increasing need to not be home. At this point, there is little understanding, little time spent together, and little conversation. Consequently, the young family member who was once worth disciplining is quickly reconstituted or given a new identity, in light of increased absence and increased problem behavior. Such a reconstitution can be extremely significant if the individual becomes involved in further out-of-home problems (e.g., police, school, etc.), since this serves to confirm parent suspicions about problem behavior, using the definitions of social control agents to do so.

> *No school, no marks, no money, no nothing! We weren't talking in my house. Mom said that she had nothing to say. [emphasis] period! That I had better get the message. Then I get popped (arrested) for fuckin' around in the trains. I knew that was it!*
>
> *Respondent number 23*

Considering the above accounts, it can be hypothesized that absence becomes a personal choice once young people define their relationship viz-a-viz family members as problematic.

Friends As Role Models

One of the first encounters for young people drifting out of home is their friends. Most young people initially viewed their friends as simply people they like to be with. This might be expected, since prior to the onset of any feeling of drift, friends are important parts of everyday life. In most cases, friends were mentioned as either having been seen daily in school or work, or as having backgrounds, interests and concerns similar to those of the individual. However, beyond the issues of similarity and sharing, young people often spoke about two other dimensions tied to friends: these being the friend as the problem and friends as examples of runaway behavior.

In many cases, daily contact with particular friends was a continual irritant to parents. Either one or both parents were reported to have continually viewed their children's contact with certain friends as taboo, as noted in the quote below. Often, this feeling of parents was not supported by any actual observation of unacceptable behavior.

> *My mother just said that was one person who she could never trust. I asked her why she felt that way and she just continued to tell me she had no trust. She didn't really give me an answer, she just continued to talk. Without any sort of reason, my parents go and put the finger on this one guy for me getting arrested outside school. I told them that he wasn't even there! They said to me, why not? I said 'cause he was sick that day.' They said that was some more bullshit and that he probably was smart enough to walk away before the cops got there.*
>
> *Respondent number 24*

When the friend or group of friends are a continual irritant, this causes a polarization between parent and child over being at home versus being with friends. This friction adds to any already existing problem. Here again, a type of process can be identified, in that the issue of choosing friends is ceremonially made into an either them or us situation. Prior to this, parents might not be fond of their children's companions; however, an ultimatum has not yet been presented. But when this does occur, many young people are forced to choose between a home situation they feel a certain disinterest toward or friends who, at the minimum, provide peer support.

This could be viewed as an easy choice to make; yet in many cases young persons aren't really in a position to know what to do about their predicament. Leaving home could be reflected on but the reality of the situation isn't yet realized. Almost all youths spoke about running away as not being perceived as a posibility until they saw others leave home because of problems like their own. Friends are often viewed as examples of how to run away. Wanting to escape home may be a vague idea up until this point, however, once a role model appears, what once appeared vague quickly becomes focused. Several statements made by respondents clearly establish the importance of role models.

> *I never really did think much about moving out until I see this guy Ralph do it. Nothing happened to him, he just left. I thought the cops would get him but nobody bothered him. I've been out three weeks now and I ain't been back, don't want to go back. Things is just fine. Now had you asked me before leaving, I would not know what to say but now that I see everybody doing it, I say why not me?*
>
> *Respondent number 2*

> *I talked about this problem at school. Once a month I would speak with the guidance lady. I would talk about what was going on in the school and at home. She asked me if I wanted her to call up my folks, I said no! She said she did not want me leaving home! I said why would I do that? She said, well some kids do that, you know. I thought she was fooling me.*
>
> *Respondent number 15*

Examples set by peers seem to be an essential prerequisite to running away for two reasons. First, they tend to confirm the already vague feeling or need to believe that something can be done about a situation (e.g., leave home—that there is somthing others who are having problems have done). Second, they provide survival information or techniques on how somebody makes it once he or she leaves home. An underlying assumption in this investigation is that, for the most part, conventional, in-home behavior does not prepare someone for the out-of-home experience. Thus, it is crucial that some initial example exist for a person to follow. Friends often serve that purpose.

The Right Situation

The decision to leave often becomes crystalized around the occurrence of the right situation. A right situation can perhaps best be characterized as a situation where the youth is either in extreme turmoil and conflict or extreme passivity. Such extreme situations seem to generate running away because they limit any constructive dialogue and young people thus feel justified in leaving. All respondents reported their point of view as a question of justice. No one left home for the sake of leaving, but rather because life had become too problematic. As pointed out by one young man:

> *I wasn't about to sit around there and be yelled at and messed with. I didn't do nothing that bad. My mother said she was going to court with me so what was I supposed to do? She just kept yelling and yelling about court. What was I gonna say? I don't want to go to no court.*
>
> *Respondent number 17*

However, this interpretation of the situation was often a matter of the style the young person used in a problem home setting. Some young people, for example, suggested that they were more assertive than others during at home conflicts and this assertion often resulted in a worsening of matters, because neither the parent nor the child would back down. The result was that the young person left home. This contrasts with the more passive person who, not being totally sure of leaving, would "back off" from the situation and try to figure out what to do next. Both types, however, beyond the question of leaving, recognized that things were, in the words of one young woman, "getting bad." She noted:

> *I wasn't about to do anything different from what I usually did, so I just waited. But you know, I kinda figured people would jump all over me again, so I right then and there figured that I would have to get out of here or else it would be more of the same.*
>
> *Respondent number 16*

Sometimes the situation wasn't viewed as an extreme by a respondent. However, its repetitions signaled that relations were growing worse.

> *We used to have these like rap sessions. They started coming almost every night. I figured that since we were gonna be talking every night that my father would eventually get the idea that I was getting high and kick my ass. I sort of didn't think it was worth talking about so I started getting ready to leave.*
>
> *Respondent number 14*

During the course of this investigation, no overall standard was identified regarding when the right situation for leaving home clearly exists. However, many young people reported that right situations occurred when little discussion or negotiation could take place, and the potential for resolving any problem was minimized.

Shrinking Alternatives

The desire to leave and the actual act of leaving home were often consequences of what I term here as shrinking alternatives -- alternatives could shrink as a result of different problems and scenarios.

To what degree alternatives were viewed as "shrinking" depended upon their immediate consequences. A comparison of statements on what were perceived as possible benefits to leaving home illustrate this point.

> *My mother decided we would be better off in court. So her, me and my sister were going there. My mother had called the cops prior to this and they told her she ought to go to the court and make a complaint. My sister was in support of her, so I figured it was either me or them!*
>
> *Respondent number 16*

> *The way I figured it, I was supposed to do one of three things; stop seeing my boyfriend, stop seeing him on weekdays, or get out of the*

house. Much of the problem was about drugs.
I used to get high, you know. First everybody
was pretty okay. I mean, they were upset, but
helpful. They wanted to talk. When that didn't
work, the next thing was to go to a shrink.
There's a place in Sutphin Boulevard that
don't cost a lot. I went there. That wasn't
much help, so I started going to the drug
programs, you know rap sessions, etc. I mean I
tried different things, it was different. I think
my folks figured things would get better. No
more dope. Well after about a year, they
started to get pissed, I had gone through all
this shit and still no change. My old man said
he was going to call the cops, have me put
away. By then things really changed. There
was just no more chances, so I left.

Respondent number 16

The three comments listed above demonstrate that possible alternative actions became almost non-existent. All three situations were problematic and the youths involved found no room for discussion with their families.

Based on the data collected, it appears that as long as the police, doctors or other authorities were not brought into the family setting, the family could work toward a resolution. However, in some instances, the alternatives were non-existent as in the case of the family court being involved. Once the court was involved in the problem, it was no longer a localized family issue. The family itself could no longer make choices, but rather it was the court and the family making or seeking alternatives. Respondent statements show that when this occurred, the situation was totally redefined because family could no longer guarantee or control outcomes.[2]

Most young people spoke casually about relations at home in this type of situation. In many cases, even in the face of shrinking alternatives, the young person claimed to "know his parents" and know what they would do. However, once some third party such as a court became involved, young people often felt that long-standing feelings had been cast aside on behalf of some sort of outside resolution. Once that occurred, some youth felt the best way to protect themselves was to flee the setting.

The First Impressions of the Absentee

Even after the decision to leave, feelings about home, conventional home routines, past problems, etc., are still unsettled. Many young people felt disorganized about what they did, as evidenced by several quotes.

> *I was afraid about what happened, but I knew I couldn't stay there (home). After like two days at a friend's, I called my brother and he told me to come home so we could talk.*
>
> *Respondent number 1*

> *I was glad I left but not so glad about staying away. You know, like it was different.*
>
> *Respondent number 1*

> *If my father had been there I probably would never have left. The more I thought, the more that bothered me. I couldn't do much, except think about whether leaving was a good thing.*
>
> *Respondent number 11*

> *Right after I left, that night I called up my brother and returned.*
>
> *Respondent number 11*

Although some young people had no "second thoughts" about their decision,[3] most wanted to be sure they had done the right thing. "Being sure" most often implied checking back with siblings, friends, etc., if they were close enough to home. At first, this was a fairly easy thing to do since most runners knew where to locate brothers and sisters.

Some respondents even reported using brothers and sisters to re-enter the house during the day to gather up personal items left behind earlier. However, beyond the matter of mixed feelings, some respondents reported a certain feeling about "freedom of choice" that was guarded by being "outside the home and alone." As was suggested by one person:

111

As nervous as I was about not being in the
house, dealing with the cops, money, etc., I
was glad to be out of there!
Respondent number 3

For respondents who remained away (some reported
returning: see last chapter), the challenge adjusting to a new
situation quickly turned into a problem of sustaining one's
self in a new situation. Young people away from home for
the first time have to make choices — choices which often
demonstrate the reality of functioning for the first time as
an independent human being. Much like divorcees or persons
recently separated in a marriage, runaways find that old routines often become awkward in new situations. Consequently, for runaways, the issue is deciding about how old routines
fit into the new pattern of living away from home. For
example, most persons interviewed reported conflict between
the need of attending school and the fact that the friend they
were staying with had quit. This is awkward because unless
a runaway leaves school, persons befriending the youth by
giving shelter are not receiving the benefit and camaraderie of
his or her all day presence. There is also conflict involved in
going to school when a young person away from home is
being sought after by parents. Since many runaways were
unprepared for an encounter with parents (via school), most
typically decided to forget school and remain with friends.

In some cases, school difficulties were the reason for
leaving home, so attending school wasn't problematic. However, other matters were; such as, curiosity about what is
occurring at home, continuation at a particular job, a continued contact with older brothers or sisters, etc. This is the
first instance that any young person has to consider the
choice between some of the routines found in the in-home
setting versus those demanded while out of the home.

In the previous chapter, we considered a number of
different events reported by young people as constituting a
day. As a heuristic device, it is helpful to think of these as
either conventional or unconventional activities. For example, most young people of fourteen years of age are in
school and living at home—this is so partly because of con-
ventionality and mostly through statute. The state has, on
behalf of a child's welfare, made school attendance compul-

112

sory at this age. Thus, a fourteen year old is expected to be in school. In a home setting, we expect such conventional routines and concerns to be upheld.

Because of interest as guardians and also due to legal requirements, parents are responsible for their children's presence in school. However, in the out-of-home setting, parental responsibility for and concern about school attendance is missing and there are other concerns that take precedence over school. This is usually not because education isn't a concern to the new runaway from home. In fact, many of the young people interviewed mentioned school and felt the need to justify their absence from it. However, the longer a young person remains out of school, the lower a priority it takes and identity with this type of conventional student role weakens. Consider these remarks:

> *School, well I've been going as much as I can go. I'm afraid that if I stay out, there will be more trouble.*
>
> *Respondent number 1*

> *School? No, I don't go (laughter). (Out of home one and a half years)*
>
> *Respondent number 30*

As documented by the above comments, the concern about school fades out. The making of such choices might be looked upon as a managing of residual activities. Because the gradual shift in interests that range from tolerating the home to remaining away from it, there may be some continuation of "in-home" concerns. However, it is increasingly important that these residuals be managed successfully, if the young person becomes more familiar and capable with out-of-home concerns.

Another example of managing a residual activity is runaway programs that work with families in resolving absence problems. Many families rely on these programs to assist them in keeping their children from running away again, or in safe quarters if already away from home. Under parental direction, a young person often establishes some sort of contact or friendship in this program setting and goes to the program for help. Rap sessions, temporary resi-

113

dence and medical attention are the sorts of services provided to young people there.

Once a young person decides to leave home, however, parents often expect the program to locate their child and talk the child into returning home. This is a residual issue for young people, since it represents something engaged in prior to leaving home. In order to clearly move toward the path of continued absence, this situation must be successfully managed by the young person. This means being able to explain prior contacts, friendships, etc., made in these programs either to himself or to the circle of peers who listen as interested parties once he's away from home. Going back to the program for assistance could imply a willingness to return home—since this often is what the program believes is the best alternative.

To successfully run away, all residual issues need to be put into proper perspective. Not to do so leaves an individual still very much tied to the home setting that he or she is supposed to be leaving. Runaway programs reported a great deal of ambivalence among young people about completely cutting ties to their homes. The first days away from home are often spent deciding whether the choice is worth making. The following quote from a runaway program worker highlights this indecision.

> *Like almost anything else, people don't always know what's out here. You have to be out to see how it feels; then you can make choices. I suppose that is why you got so many kids running back and forth, not sure about themselves.*
>
> *Youth Worker, New York City*

The concept of knowing one's self is also important in the first days away from home. Most young persons interviewed were not very sure of themselves, especially in areas pertaining to material support.

Contrasting statements made by newly arrived absentees versus those away for at least six months, one finds the veterans are more certain about living arrangements, support, the law, the feeling of returning home and what they will be doing in the near future. Thus, young people do, in the course of their absence away from home, learn how to perform in this new role of runaway. This transition that occurs in a youth's understanding of self after continued absence is probably best viewed as perfecting the runaway role.

Learning and Refining the Runaway Role

As was already suggested, becoming a runaway involves learning how and what is expected in such a role. Based upon both interviews and observations, it appears that a runaway role can best be understood in terms of several themes that make it unique from other identities. To occupy a runaway role and later embrace a runaway identity is to set oneself apart from someone who is merely away temporarily. Themes that concern runners and make up their day need to be learned, resolved or ignored if the runaway is to continue making it. "Making it" implies that few problems or obstacles are present in somebody's life away from home and in this investigation, "making it" was voiced by respondents as a major theme.

There are two issues within the "making it" theme. One issue concerns itself with the basic matter of "how well is the person holding his own while away?" The second concern is quality of life. The first issue is viewed as a very conventional concern, because young people often spoke about finding jobs, checking out jobs, school, living with friends, girlfriends, boyfriends, etc., on behalf of "making it". The term conventional is used here since these sorts of issues show little difference in emphasis from those in a conventional situation. Much of the initial behavior of absentees is very conventional (i.e., should I stay with friends or not, etc.). As suggested by one person:

> *My first day, hey, you know I was sort of worried about a place to stay, better than the one I had, things like that. There wasn't no problems or excitement or things like that. I just sort of was searching things out.*
> *Respondent number 9*

However, once a young person moves beyond initial concerns or several of the above mentioned residual issues he or she brings from home, there are new choices to be

115

made that begin to move him or her in other less conventional directions. The second issue involved in the "making it" theme, the quality of life, is involved here.

In summary, what does the person have to do to "make it," and what does it get him? The vast majority of the people talked with were willing and eager to seek out work, school opportunities, etc. Most were familiar with the sorts of problems talked about without education, etc. However, most were also very aware of the continued lack of progress of either themselves or friends in trying to make it in school or work as runaways. One remedy to this was to try new methods that would allow one to make it without too many problems, or as one person said: to really get over[1]

"Getting Over"

The term "getting over" was provided by one of my respondents in the course of our meetings. His personal decision to "get over" in everything he does exemplifies the runaway's desire to make it while doing little in order to insure such a successful outcome. The "getting over" could be thought of as an ideology. The "getting over" ideology supports a number of concrete behaviors, or what I earlier referred to as hustles. The most common are related to drugs, sex, theft and various flim-flamming activities. Although one could equate "getting over" behavior with laziness, carefree living, etc., runaways' comments and my own observations do not support this theory. If anything, then, the hallmark of the getting over ideology is illegality *rather* than easy carefree living.

For example, among the respondents I spoke with, the low-level, drug-selling market in New York City was portrayed as hard work. Various concerns, exemplified by the comments of one spokesperson, tend to support this thought.

> *Sure I sell some drugs to different people, all sorts of drugs and to tell you again it's kinda risky. But I got other problems than risk you know. I've got to worry about my own supplies, that nobody ain't rippin me off. I have to worry about cash, all that! Plus I got to continue to look good to my own people and not lose money. I always got to make sure the*

*money is there and that I look good. To do
all this, I have to really move around. . .all the
time.*

Respondent number 9

How someone appears to regular friends while engaged
in a "getting over" lifestyle is important, as exemplified by
statements concerning drugs:

*I need to make sure what I get people is popu-
lar, you know hip. Certain drugs ain't hip.
Like people get real uptight and hustle behind
Angel Dust. The word is out that I don't want
to play with that cause people wouldn't dig it.
My friends wouldn't dig it.*

Sometimes, making it through illicit means such as
drugs can backfire. This was demonstrated in the case where
several people living together refused to allow the drug sale
activity to proceed from their temporary quarters. Guilt by
association is a typical concern here since a drug "sale"
arrest in New York State, when one is over the age of sixteen, can be a serious matter. Many adolescents recognize
the dangers associated with selling drugs for profit.

The Redefinition of Urgency

The habit of viewing things as being urgent changes as
one becomes more and more involved in the out-of-home
experience. Concerns and matters once viewed as a crisis,
or something in need of immediate management, become remote or out-of-date. Many young people talked about court
or school in the past tense without a sense of urgency or an
expression of intimidation. The interpretation could be made
that when someone remains away long enough, former concerns become irrelevant. They become replaced by other
concerns which are common to people who have decided
to leave or were forced out of their homes.

When I explored typical issues of urgency with respondents, most suggested that they were not a problem
since they no longer felt confusion or fear about going

117

home. They were caught between two difficult choices; one that represented home and one that represented independence. Although some young people were not articulate on this point, some gave indications that supported this notion. For example, one person reported the continued urgency driven into him while at home to attend the youth program prescribed by the family court. This urgency grew and his older brother even escorted him to the program daily in order to insure his arrival! From this youth's standpoint, this urgency was no longer necessary since he was now responsible for his own timetable and actions.

Considering this redefinition process viz-a-viz other events thus far mentioned in the transformation to a runaway identity, it may be that this makes things more workable or palatable to runners. That is, when we contrast the demands of a runaway setting with that of a home setting, we see that urgency may not be important. In fact, rather than urgency, a certain degree of patience seems important, as demonstrated by one person commenting on work:

> *You know, I go down to look for jobs every day. Something that will give me some money, like a job that will let you learn something, but No Job. I guess you just got to wait it out.*
> *Respondent number 29*

There was one exception to this rule with respect to the reduced emphasis on urgency which appeared most often among the hustlers. Several of the young people I interviewed were involved daily in hustles. Each hustler varied in his purpose or style, but each placed an emphasis on swiftness, coolness,[4] and calculation. This was especially true of the drug-related hustlers since they were often preoccupied with safety, meeting connections, buying drugs, selling drugs, etc. Since these participants were business types, the emphasis was on making profits and minimizing problems. "Viewing everything as urgent" is a theme which characterized the drug hustlers' perception of the world. For them, the new problem was keeping things "together" for the drug hustle. By doing this, independence was assured through making money and constant contact with new people.

Perfection

The final theme which is characteristic of someone's involvement and transformation in a runaway environment is "perfection." Each of the young people spoken with wished to improve his or her lot and no one viewed his present situation as the most desirable. Young people, for instance, when questioned about living arrangements, often said they were on shaky ground. The need to improve such a situation was a regular preoccupation. This might be viewed as a case of seeking perfection.

Perfection was especially important to the young people who were heavily involved in the illegal networks of drug hustling or body hustling. Here, perfection means making increasing amounts of money, not risking being set up by rivals or friends, not being beaten up by strangers. Not all young people thought in terms of being perfect, but rather in terms of improvement. An example of such a range can be seen in comments made by three respondents on the issue of improving their station in life.

I'd like to be sure I could stay here for a long while (improvement in 'temporary' residence).

My own place would be the best, without that kind of moving in and out shit (improvement on 'regular' residence).

I would hope to get an apartment and so then me and my friend could be tight. You know, get married. (Improvement of both residence and present friendship).

The above comments suggest we could think of living requirements as falling within a hierarchy, based upon the permanence of the situation, the security or safety in the situation, and the variety of companionship in the situation.

Another example of a hierarchy would be with respect to where people hang out. Many young people reported at first staying in many of the same places they frequented while home; that is, schools, school yards, train stations, recreation centers, crisis, youth development or runaway

119

centers they typically visited. They stayed at these places with many of the same friends they had while at home. However, as time away from home increases, both the vicinity and friends tend to change. For instance, many young people who recently left home spoke of going back to the vicinity near their school to either see friends or siblings. Such young people were vague or even undecided about what they had been doing or would do to settle other matters. In contrast, people away for over six months often spoke of specific nightspots or vicinities for hustles as the preferred alternative to hanging out near home.

As a whole, these themes could be viewed as an anatomy of a runaway role. As was noted above, they exist in, and activities related to them are engaged in, to varying degrees. However, despite this variability, anyone who wants to remain absent from his home must consider these factors. Such factors are what youths away from home deem as the minimum for survival—and by pursuing such minimums, one's status as a runaway is solidified; one's identity as a runner emerges.

Performance in Role, Confirmation and Confidence

The final phase in the transformation process of being able to view one's self as a runaway is seen in the peer judgments made about performance. Thus, the ultimate step toward an unconventional lifestyle is being certain that a youth can perform well in the runaway role—that is, that there is an alternative and that it is defined as socially real.

Peer Judgment and Performance

As was noted by one young person: "how you feel about yourself is a lot of times tied to what your friends feel about you." Slightly translated, the ultimate judgment about someone's attempt in the runaway role is made by his peers. Within this investigation, the notion of a peer was difficult to define since the definition of a peer changes with the situation and the amount of time away from home. For instance, for someone recently out of his home, the primary peer reference group is the neighborhood friends he or she had while living at home. Very often, opinions or judgments about what or how well someone is doing is based upon their own major reference point or criterion — the home. Until this point then, discussion, feelings or opinions about performance are home bound. The significance of this factor is twofold. First, many young people felt that friends were supportive but viewed them as losers or persons with little support. Second, these feelings postponed the learning of any of the basic themes found in a runaway role or a feeling of making it out-of-the-home.

In contrast, for young people reporting absence of more than a six month period, both the peer references and criteria for judgments are different. Young people away from home at this point often report increased reliance on themselves, new friends and contacts, welfare offices, crash pads, runaway programs or, in some cases, temporary one-day flop house arrangements. Several events reinforce such developments, among these were increased mistrust of friends, the need to seek out more realistic means of support, as well as freedom and curiosity. Along with this, the judgment criterion a person uses about his absence from home also changes. It no longer is based upon home concerns but on out-of-home concerns. Thus, someone becomes judged not on the everyday matters of school attendance, amount of contact with parents, a respect for the urgency with which parental demands must be met or home security but, rather, realistic living arrangements (does he have them?), is he "making it" (a job or hustle), does he have a clear picture about the possibility of returning home, etc. In a sense, a young person begins to judge others on the themes which are common to all actors in the runaway network.

Regular Contact and a Runaway Social Circle

The final stage in this transformation process is the establishment of a regular pattern of contact. This is viewed as the point when an individual begins to prearrange his activities, set up expectations around the runaway role and, in turn, views others as doing the same. Once an individual begins to plan, a degree of reciprocity sets in. This development may be looked upon as a regular contact with a runaway social circle. Based upon interview data collected in this investigation, there is not a pattern in which people become increasingly involved in such a runaway social circle. Several respondents reported that such involvement included with it a continued pursuit of the themes outlined above as well as a collective planning for these pursuits.

The runaway social circle may be defined as made up of loosely-connected individuals, sensitive to both the day-to-day routine of being out of home as well as the extremes of such lifestyles. The everyday routine of the runaway life-style requires an awareness of not only what needs do occur daily but what must never occur. Consistent action, as well as an appreciation for extremes, can only be realized through a regular contact. As was put by one respondent:

> *If you want to hang with certain people, you got to know how to act. You don't be stupid, you need to be smart. Like if you go into a store, you don't start boosting shit (steal) if you don't know where you are. That type of stuff is crazy. There are hippier ways to get things done—and people always want to hang with an 'easy dude.'*
> *Respondent number 29*

An "easy dude" (mentioned in the above quote) is a person who recognizes a risk or extreme and the do's and don'ts of a runaway social circle. In a general sense, becoming a runaway is dependent upon what others have viewed you as able to do—or to put it in the popular jargon —"where you're at."

> *People need to know where you are at. See, cause it ain't no use making plans with some-body you know you can't trust, somebody who's gonna use you.*
> *Respondent number 8*

Participants in the loosely affiliated runaway circle understand these rules and to that extent this social setting is seen as structured by rules. No one spoke about rules per se, but every respondent who reported a regular and pat-terned routine was able to point to friends whom they trusted and who are aware of what to do. This is important in understanding how someone becomes committed to the runaway social circle. Once a pattern is established, individual youths often appear to become tied or dependent upon each other. They appear to accommodate each other emotionally, sexually, materially, and/or in the exchange of information. In short, they help each other cope even though in some circumstances, each may be suspicious of the other. A woman respondent noted:

> *Once I decided to leave my boyfriend, I didn't have it all figured out how I would live. . .that is, since I was gonna leave, anyway, I decided to come down here for a while (temporary runaway residence). I knew about the place through several of the people we would hang with so I figured it would be okay since I knew the people.*
>
> *Respondent number 32*

Helping others sometimes takes place in physically threatening situations as in the case of a sixteen-year-old female seeking sanctuary from rivals in the South Bronx.

> *I just decided I was gonna have to get out of this neighborhood quick. These guys know me and know where to find me, so I just hooked up with some old friends out of the neighborhood.*
>
> *Respondent number 32*

This type of limited comradeship may, at times, be linked to other sorts of social networks. A prime example of this is the drug hustlers. Since, in many cases, some of the same people who rely on drugs are hustlers themselves and also know of other illegal but adjunct activities. They sometimes are gatekeepers of valuable information.

> *These two people I was staying with sometimes would let me cop drugs for them. So I would be doing this so they themselves wouldn't get taken off—you know white dudes sometimes do. Anyway, one looks like she got hepatitis (Hep) or something and she don't know it. I tell her she better have it checked out—but she was afraid to. I looked up all the informa-*

tion for her through my own drug connection.
Respondent number 13

The continually increased reinforcement of and preoccupation with the runaway social circle gives a person a sense that he or she is part of this unconventional world. Such a feeling as it is reinforced daily by new friends, new problems and new themes makes it increasingly easy to speak and think of oneself as a *"long time participant"* or *"somebody who's got confidence."*

> *The real important thing when somebody leaves home is to know what you will do. You don't. That's why you do the same old thing. Once you move around, you get some confidence—you get to know yourself, you get to see how people treat you and others like you.*
> *Respondent number 13*

Once a person feels confidence, a sense of control emerges. By controlling a situation, the person can either choose to continue the involvement in the present routine or attempt to return to a conventional lifestyle. Several young persons talked about returning; however, they did so in only a sketchy sense. One spoke about being a little "embarrassed" to speak about some of the bad things that had happened in the last year. This tends to block off the possibility of returning home.

The same individual pointed out that he would probably not return home anyway but would rather live with his aunt and uncle. He noted:

> *That's real shit going back there. I've talked to my brother and he told me the same thing is going on.*
> *Respondent number 11*

In a sense, the fact that someone can "think twice" about going home may signal the fact that this new world or lifestyle has taken on a new meaning and new obligations and new values. The individual who is really away is now able to stake a claim and can do so by involving others like

124

himself, a process that Becker (1960) has described:

> . . .commitment has been achieved by making *a side bet*. The committed person has acted in such a way as to involve other interests of his . . .directly in that action. By his own actions prior to the final bargaining session, he has staked something of value to him, something originally unrelated to his present line of action, on being consistent in his present behavior. (p. 37).

In this view, we can see that the bond between the runaway social circle and the individual becomes strengthened.

I have, then, argued that various activities established in-the-home gradually become replaced by other activities out-of-the-home. I will next examine these same progressive steps in a runaway's development from the specific conceptual viewpoint of the career perspective.

CHAPTER FOOTNOTES

[1] See Dennis Brisset, *Toward an Interactionist Understanding of Heavy Drinking*, for a somewhat similar discussion concerning this.

[2] The inclusion of outside parties makes original agreements null and void.

[3] This was typical among young people whom I observed to be indifferent about most things. (See the next chapter on the typology concerning the different types of runaways.)

[4] Irwin also identified coolness as a quality important to a hustler (See *The Felon*, Prentice Hall, 1970).

CHAPTER VII

THE CAREER PERSPECTIVE

As was suggested in Chapter I, a primary task here is to understand the value of a career perspective in analyzing running away from home and define who is a runaway. This investigation has continually made reference to a career as it provides a better base for understanding the transformation from an in-home to an out-of-home identity. Further, it sharpens our sense of how this process is identified by actors themselves.

The process of becoming a runaway may be likened to Lemert's statement about personal shifts from primary to secondary deviance "the secondary deviant. . .is a person whose life and identity are organized around the facts of deviance" (Lemert: 1951). In this chapter an identification and analysis of the respective stages of the runaway experience will be undertaken. We will focus on how each set of out-of-home events allows the individual to become further immersed in the out-of-home experience. . .and ultimately into the runaway role.

The process and general stages by which someone comes to be recognized by others as a runaway is formally depicted and outlined in this chapter. The runaway process can be viewed as having two conceptual components: (1) stages that individuals pass through which are typical to children away from home, and (2) personal styles which allow individuals to grow more concerned about a runaway routine. In using these two components, I hope to account for both the individual and collective events which are central to the runaway experience. Moreover, we will try to account for those many instances where children retreat from or reject the runaway scene and return home.

As a prelude to exploring runaway stages, it is important that brief consideration be given to several understandings regarding a runaway career. First, individuals encounter and are confronted with out-of-home experiences in different ways and in different combinations. Children bring distinct viewpoints to those events, encounters and interactions they find outside home. For example, some children are less concerned with independence and more concerned with fun. For some children, leaving home is just another excitement episode. Second, children leaving home must work to master the events of the runaway situation in order to remain in it. This can be seen as a movement from a primary to a secondary deviance. Independent of any personal capability (i.e., toughness, confidence, etc.) they bring to the runaway situation, that situation presents a new set of contingencies or problems which must be overcome. In the course of doing this investigation, a variety of people were encountered. For example, some runaways were more aware of the stakes and their personal danger. Other young people were not. However, despite personal diversity, a unifying issue for each person was to establish certainty about their new status out of the home. Children were constantly reviewing any sense of dependence and modifying any daily problem or obstacle viewed as a threat to their daily activity. This activity of working to master the runaway scene can be viewed as attempting to create an end product or "product in process," and can be understood as the centralizing issue of a runaway lifestyle. Young people out of their homes are constantly examining, evaluating and revising cues given by others in connection with the out-of-home experience. To be a runaway can only be accomplished after a long sequence of interaction that moves the person from some "primary" involvement to a more routine secondary involvement. As Lemert (1951) has noted concerning the person's movement from a primary to a secondary deviance:

> The sequence of interaction leading from primary to secondary deviation is roughly as follows: (1) primary deviation; (2) social penalties; (3) further primary deviation; (4) stronger penalties and rejections; (5) further deviation, perhaps with hostilities and resentment beginning to focus upon those doing the

penalizing; (6) crisis reached in the tolerance quotient, expressed in formal action by the community stigmatizing of the deviant; (7) strengthening of the deviant conduct as a re-action to the stigmatizing and penalties; (8) ultimate acceptance of deviant social status and efforts at adjustment on the basis of the asso-ciated role. (Lemert 1951)

In the present discussion of runaways, the movement from a primary to secondary style is dependent upon recog-nizing, learning, and routinizing home concerns. It is to these concerns that we now turn to and the respective stages within which they unfold.

Out of Home Concerns

Passing from conventional role into the runaway role is a trial and error process. It requires involvement, learning, reinforcement and growth. Yablonsky, in his description of Synanon and its work with drug addicts, provides an excel-lent portrayal of the steps individuals pass through in moving from the "drug" scene to the "Synanon" scene. He notes: ". . .Synanon provides (1) an interesting social setting. . .with associates who understand the person; (2) an opportunity structure. . .with legitimate possibility for achievement and prestige; (3) a new role that can indefinitely occupy the process of social growth; (4) social growth, somewhat a personal recognition that the person is able to relate, com-municate and work with others."

For children away from home, the social audiences they encounter often supply them with the settings, support and opportunity to become immersed into a runaway life-style. Recall in the last chapter the theme of "friends as examples." Having friends who have already left home or friends as sympathizers sets up a temporary social setting similar to the setting found in Synanon. However, friends are but one concrete concern children confront when away, there are many other concerns. In interviewing and observ-ing young persons out of their homes, there exists at least three distinct concerns reported in the process of becoming a runaway. These include (1) the fear of reversal; (2) being accepted and "appearing right;" (3) the freedom of choice.

128

Most young persons constantly struggled with these matters while away. Operationally, we may view observations about problems as a basis for understanding at what stage the young person is in the runaway career. Further, by learning what young people report about these concerns, we can determine if any serious identification of a runaway role or commitment to a runaway career has occurred. The runaway role is viewed here as something that is manufactured in the cause of social interaction. Becoming immersed in the below mentioned concerns is synonymous with some degree of commitment to the runaway role and some personal location along a runaway career.

The Fear of Reversal

One concern voiced by young people is the possible need to reverse or change their activities. Reversals take two forms; going home or going in "new directions." Going home is a return to home and parental authority. Going in "new directions" implies some involvement in illegal drugs, sex, or theft operations. Unfortunately, once out of the home, the career path young people follow is not always clear. Since neither going home or illegal behavior are the preferred options, the choices young people make are difficult. However, changes and choices are often necessary as being away from home is often a set of "tentative" or temporary experiences, as can be seen from the comments about everyday residence.

> *Well, in the past ten days I have made six changes. I sure wish I could get a regular place to stay. The first two days I stayed with Larry (friend) but that cancelled out. From last week its been the train, the YMCA and the shelter. I don't like the shelter, so I'm not staying there.*
>
> *Respondent number 10*

> *I've got till the end of the month to pay up on the place, after that who knows.*

> *Hey, in New York you can do about anything . . .you just got to keep moving. . .moving*

sucks, but that's the way it is now.

If I could get my play on some blow (co-caine). . .I'd be okay. . .CASH is the thing. If you have some money, you can stay around and get yourself together. You see a job, meet some people. . .make this a regular thing. I think this is better than the Brooklyn House (foster care) but I ain't saying for sure.
Respondent number 20

The runaway career, unlike conventional occupational careers, does not provide straight paths or regular opportunities for growth. Some young people find it necessary to return home only to again leave when the correct opportunity presents itself. As young people are attempting to establish themselves, evaluation of everyday risks and dangers can cause shifts in thinking about returning home, or engaging in behavior that would otherwise be seen as dangerous to the young person. Moreover, the out-of-home experience, like other "deviant" lifestyles, is often characterized by limited resources and risks not always totally understood or recognized by the person exploring the runaway role. Contingencies like the lack of shelter, money, safety or friends can make the process of running away a very uncertain one. Luckenbill and Best (1981) have succinctly described the problems contained in the deviant career by contrasting it to conventional career paths individuals follow. They note:

The differences between deviant and respectable careers are consequential for deviants. Developing within a less clearly structured context, with comparatively few institutional supports, deviant careers feature individualized career shifts rather than standard sequences of positions. Decisions to make career shifts reflect special career contingencies: deviants risk apprehension and sanctioning by the authorities; they face betrayal or exploitation by deviant associates; the rewards from deviant activities are unstable and irregular;

and the supply of resources needed for deviance is difficult to control. These contingencies contribute to the uncertainty of the deviant experience. Deviants respond by leaving deviance or devising tactics for managing uncertainty and insuring career security.

Some choose to leave deviance. Whereas respectable careers generally extend over the individual's working life, deviant careers vary in length. Some people quit deviance after a single episode and others leave after a few years; relatively few make it a lifelong commitment. (Luckenbill and Best 1981 202)

Indeed, even when young people report themselves as comfortable and capable of surviving out of their homes, the need to further specify their future is reflected on, as noted in the following

> *Yes, I've been out here for eleven months now. . .but I need something more solid. . . I've been visiting my cousin and he is gonna set up a regular job for me. . .I'd rather not play in the streets. . .that's bullshit. . .but with nothing else jumping off, I guess I'll lay here.*
>
> *Respondent number 7*

Being Accepted and Appearing Right

Given the strangeness and novelty of the out of home experience, it is often difficult to estimate the progress a person is making.

The out of home experience can prove to be a trying time in a young person's life. A host of new experiences are encountered and this often serves to influence how individuals will be socially defined. Young people will either "make it" or flounder. Running may be viewed as an occasion for developing the skills to be viewed as important to the runaway role. Skills are important to a young person, since they provide a base from which one's self is located viz-a-viz social worlds. For example, the ability to exchange old friendships with new friendships, or the ability to spot "trouble" in mixed company. Luckenbill and Brill have noted the difficulty experienced by individuals in attempting to locate themselves with a runaway career; "deviant careers, with their minimal structure, secrecy and diverse career shifts are more difficult to interpret. In retrospect, it may be possible to chart the direction of a deviant career; but while the career is in progress, both the deviant and others observing the career may be uncertain about its direction and outcome." (Luckinbill and Brill, 1981:202)

To perform out of the home is to develop a new self in new occasions and relationships. However, the existence of a "new self" is not automatic, especially given the quickness with which change confronts the individual out of the home. A consequence of this is that the individual must seek to establish new boundaries and understandings about where they "fit in" and an understanding of how their acts impact on the estimates of significant "others." As noted by one Brissett, "One of the crucial and sometimes excruciating pursuits of people is to establish their individuality (Brissett, 1978:9). Being socially defined as a runaway offers an opportunity to locate one's self. Being seen as a "runner" sets one apart from the nebulous adolescent experience and allows the individual to be seen in a different light. The process of being typed as a runaway allows one to "set one's mark" and to do this is to be part of a select group. To be part of such an experience is to have achieved what Stone (1962) has termed "appearance." One appears a certain way to other in interaction and thus they can be located by others—in this case as a runaway.

> One's identity is established when others place him as a social object by assigning him the same words of identity that he appropriates for himself or announces. It is in the coincidence of placements and announcements that identity becomes a meaning of the self, and often such placements and announcements are aroused by apparent symbols such as uniforms. (Stone & Faberman, 1970:399)

What becomes possible through this process is that the individual can replace uncertainty with certainty. That is, an individual can clearly mark off what is a comfortable way to perform and what a supportive social audience is. Running away may also be viewed as a means of being accepted. Upon learning what is expected in daily behavior among others, presentation of self can become a basis for acceptance. This is so since a network of friends and social contacts often grows away from home and it thus forms a base from which identification can grow. Being accepted in now always clearly achieved in the in-home adolescent routine, as young people are subordinates. The adolescent is often torn between the transition from child role to young adult role. Making choices or being pushed by adults into new choices can become problematic. The feeling of being awkward or being uncomfortable within certain "forced choice" settings can lead to feelings of being left out or being "marginally accepted." An example of this is work. Many young persons are socialized into accepting the work role and its importance in daily living. However, once in pursuit of such roles, the young find the roles elusive. While at home, few messages are received which indicate that the young person has "arrived" with respect to skill or acceptance. Being defined and locating one's self in a runaway scene can serve as a neutralizer of these experiences.

The Configuration of Activities

However, most young persons who leave home do not successfully establish a final runaway career. This is in part because the out-of-home experience is too broad and demands important shifts not always clear to the individual wishing to be a runaway. What often occurs is that young people abandon the runaway preoccupation for any set of alternative acts that will bring them money, security or approval for the moment. This marks the onset of illegal behavior in that drugs, sex and petty theft are not supports to the runaway episode but options in themselves. For example, a young person may become a hustler but by no means is a runaway.

> *The street can be a bad experience if you let it. I've been with foster parents for three years so I'm always in the street. I know how to be a player, . . .you know this runnin' shit is okay*

> *. . .but I need cash. If I can run in the street,*
> *grab a bag, move some "reefers," I'm down!*
> *Can't always afford to just hang. . .*
> > *Respondent number 36*

> *I've been here seven weeks. . .I come and go*
> *. . .I used to come here from Jersey for drugs*
> *. . .Now I hang with some guys and they take*
> *care of everything. You just can come here*
> *and survive. . .You got to have something*
> *going for you. . .you know. . .*
> > *Respondent number 23*

> *Drugs are fuckin' money. . .you know that*
> *don't you? It's quick here. . .the money*
> *turns fast. . .*
> > *Respondent number 7*

Rather than speaking about being accepted or performing a runaway role, it seems better to speak about a "configuration of roles." Young people will do what they can to remain away from home. When their out-of-home skills, activities and concerns shift from a part-time involvement to fulltime option, they are no longer moving in a runaway career.

> *Runaways. . .Hey, I don't think I know any. . .*
> *People are out here bullshitting, ripping off,*
> *copping some ass. . .You know, whatever. . .*
> *I think the papers talk that runaway shit. . .*
> *but I know lots of people who never had no*
> *place to go. . .back and forth, back and forth.*
> *Court, homes, court. . .that is a bad play. . .*
> > *Respondent number 24*

> *Hey, I'm just gonna drift as long as I can. . .*
> *and do what I can. . .*
> > *Respondent number 24*

In examining the above two quotes, it appears that many persons who remain away from home do so under any number of titles, all of which substantially draw the person into careers other than that defined as "runaway."

The Liberty of Choice

While much of what is encountered out-of-home can be problematic, it is still viewed as an opportunity for free choice. Free choice was reported as important to many people. Once away, the individual can anticipate the need and freedom to make choices. This is not to say that choices become easier to make—but they do become more person-alized. At this time, a closer fit exists between the self and the choices made to sustain one's self. This is distinct from the in-home experience which is often dictated from another person (parent, authority figure, etc.). Making choices has several implications for the actors located in the runaway scene, especially as it seems to modify the entire episode. First, daily choice requires reflection about continued par-ticipation in the runaway scene. Young people must contin-ue to reflect not only on the positive aspects of the exper-ience but also the negative. As is often the case "with free-dom comes responsibility" and the responsibility in this case always implies choice. The choice of friends, foes, shelter and support all seem to modify and contribute to the person moving forward in the career. For example, a friend's choice can spell the difference between early arrest or reinforce-ment from the runaway scene.

Second, daily choices neutralized obvious strengths and weaknesses. Despite the fact that someone may have routinized their daily existence does not mean it shall last forever. Because choice among young people must be con-stantly made, there always exists the possibility of mistakes. A mistake is a wrong choice and it often renders the person helpless or weak. Coming to the runaway scene with inordi-nate "street smarts" helps very little after a wrong choice has been made. Wrong choices make it possible for all young people regardless of social background to pass in and out of the runaway scenes. Knowing "what to say" or "what to do" is of little value if the individual makes a wrong choice. The best example of this can be seen in an earlier statement made by one young woman out-of-home and somewhat concerned about the welfare of her male companion. In this instance, the woman chose a mutually reciprocal relationship which ultimately ended in drug abuse and violence. When making

135

such a choice, the woman was obviously aware of the destructive nature of each, yet was not capable of knowing how they permeated the life of her friend.

In short, many social encounters do not provide us the background necessary to make adequate choices. However, adequate choices are at the crux of remaining away. As one continues to choose correctly, the result is reinforcement in the role. When one makes some other choice, the implication is exit or failure from the role.

Third, making choices serves as a model to peers, both with reference to the necessity of choice and the danger. With each new choice, the person either becomes more linked to the daily concerns of being away or slowly cuts the common bond. In either case, a social audience is observing and interpreting actions as they unfold.

Differential Perspective About Being Away

Not all young persons arrive at the decision to leave home for the same reasons. In this study, young persons varied in age, experience, exposure to and opinions regarding the New York City understandings about police, welfare, violence, of self-survival, verbal ability, appearance and a perspective about being away. These matters are viewed as data within this study and are termed here "perspectives."

That is, perspective places actors at various angles in relation to runaway events and influences actors to see these events from distinct angles. Perspectives tend to sensitize the individual to certain parts of physical reality, and desensitize the individual to other parts. . .they help the individual make sense of the physical reality (Charon, 1979).

In this investiagion, perspectives have come to be looked upon as important in characterizing an individual as someone who is "indifferent," "self-centered," or "peer-focused." Each of these dimensions are important to our understanding of the types of variations we find among young persons moving in and out of specific runaway stages. Although some overlap exists between these three types of young people, each can be identified as having its own particular character with respect to being away from home.

The identification of three "types" of individuals within a runaway scene takes on significance when we link each to the below stages identified within the runaway career. In doing so, it is possible to view runaway careers in concrete terms which consist of individuals trying to establish a routine for themselves out of their homes. Also, it becomes possible to have more than one "type" of runaway, since actors do bring different understanding awarenesses. It becomes possible to speak about what actors think or perceive of as critical during different phases in the out-of-home experience and what modifies such thinking. At the same time, we account for the already existing perspectives each person brings to each new social setting. In doing so, we can set some basic limits or structures with which to understand when someone views themselves as a runaway.

Indifferent Centered ("The In-Between")

These are young people who, for the most part, have no feelings about "making it as runaways." Typically, they view absence from home as "incidental" to any number of other events. For example, warrants issued by police tend to make living at home unfeasible. To be thrown out of their home via the *ad hoc* agreements between themselves, parents or other family members is another cause for absence. Such persons are typically not concerned with establishing ongoing or routine friendships on behalf of remaining away from home but will do so if necessary. They view themselves as being "in-between" lifestyles, or in a phase that they are passing through. There is no serious reflection on the future and the notion of any commitment to other people in similar predicaments is minimal. They are, as the label implies, indifferent — indifferent to work, school, friends, or absence. They place little emphasis on self in the runaway scene.

Self Centered ("The Player")

The direct opposite of the indifferent actor is the group-centered actor. This is the person who recognizes the need to stake out interests, energies and resources on behalf of not returning home. This is the person who plays out the runaway episode as entertainment. Such individuals, by necessity, are more "tuned in" to persons like themselves. They understand the implications of returning home and are willing to explore the possibilities of remaining away as a recreation form. Since many of these people see themselves looking at a "long range" rather than "in-between" life-style, relationships, resources and friendships are seen as important and not accidental. They see part of an image. There is serious reflection on the future and on an improvement of self away from home. Such individuals typically view activities like hustling or stealing as means to ends rather than ends in themselves—as part of the demanding runaway environment.

Friendship Centered ("Manipulator")

These are young persons who view themselves and their personal gains through friends, their central daily concern. Unlike the indifferent person, they want to be away. They see their situation as self-chosen, in some cases pre-planned, and in many instances, a challenge. Such individuals do not typically begin or expect to tie themselves into a runaway network. However, they often find it necessary to do so when problems develop, like losing friends. Such persons have a very clear ability to calculate the returns on any of their behaviors and many people in this category have been out of their homes in the past.

The Three Stages of Running Away

In very broad terms, the following stages can be viewed as turning points that persons pass through in order to achieve runaway status. As exemplified here, such stages might be thought of as "climactic periods" (Becker and Strauss, 1956, p. 22) during which a person's doubts, skills, activities, troubles, aspirations, etc., shift away from the concerns of the home and move towards a sense of independence from the home. In such a process, the individual comes to realize that such events are occurring, what such events imply and what significance such events play in establishing meaning out of the home. The individual realizes that there exists a behavior system which might be loosely coined a runaway scene and that he/she is, at some level, involved in it. Operationally, we recognize career stages based upon what is or is not taking place with respect to activity and how individuals are or are not coming to see the connection between their own identity and such activity. That is, what is the individual capable of doing now? How is that somehow consistent with the unifying concerns of a

138

runaway scene? How do such concerns compliment other actions? Finally, how does such a process come to confirm the feeling that someone is now a runaway?

Several earlier efforts have used a similar conceptual framework to examine the career stages of felons (Irwin, 1970), mental patients (Goffman, 1961a), drug users (Becker, 1963), and physicians (Hall, 1948). For example, Becker's (1963) view of a deviant career among marijuana users sees that the individual confronts and passes through a series of climactic developments en route to realizing the "successful" career of the marijuana user. Keeping this framework in mind, this investigation views the transformation to "runaway" as having three stages: *the unsettling stage, the exploration stage,* and *the routinization stage.* Each of these stages marks an ever increasing commitment to, awareness of and attachment to a runaway role. It should be pointed out that the events and developments which operationally mark off each of these stages are not mutually exclusive. Thus, for example, the individual who in the first days away (unsettling) spends a great deal of time in the free-association, non-structured behavior characteristic of 'hanging out,' might still find himself doing that at the latter routinization stage; yet, it will be done a great deal less. Thus, the difference is in frequency and not in kind of behavior. Operationally, this is significant, since it serves to indicate when someone is "passing" (Glaser and Strauss, 1968, p. 240) from a somewhat non-committed stage in a career to a more committed phase. Even more significant is the point when someone feels compelled to take the presence of others seriously—as something more than a trial and error adventure away from home. However, if individuals are to locate themselves in, and be considered part of the runaway scene discussed above, each stage must be passed. A person may fade in and out of such a process and it may not be linear. However, anyone who is to complete the transformation must experience each stage. Without doing so, the full meaning of events cannot be grasped and, without such a grasping, the individual cannot be fully established in their new identity.

1. The Unsettling Stage

In the very initial moments away from home, a great deal remains unsettled in the lives of absentees. At this point, someone is indeed an absentee since such a designation places him squarely within the confines of the home that he has just recently left. Implicit in this notion is the idea that one's role as a former member is still "intact," and that one might choose to resume that role if so desired. Few differences yet exists as to how someone views themselves viz-a-viz the current absence, the possibility of returning home and the realization that some alternatives may exist. In short, things are much like they were at home.

In actuality, the unsettling stage may be seen to have two parts within it. The first part has to do with the contemplation of absence; the second with the first days away from home. Data presented in Chapters IV and V would tend to support this claim. As it appears, someone must first free themselves from the burden of "not feeling justified with being away," or seeing running as an option, before they can begin to consider the unsettling realities of trying to make it away from home. For example, several young persons spoke about being reluctant to speak with brothers or sisters while contemplating absence from home since they were not yet sure they would actually leave.

As somebody moves from feeling justified about being away into facing the daily problems and contingencies connected with being away, the need for exploration increases. At this point, an individual might be seen to be passing into the next stage of the career; namely, exploration.

2. Exploratory Stage

In the same way that the unsettling stage prompts a young person into defining things as "not yet settled," the exploratory stage typically marks a phase when individuals are seeing it important to explore events around them. A typical distinction between this stage and the earlier one is that the individual has, at least for the near future, decided to remain away from home. This decision is a major reason for the need to explore since at this stage, the individual may find himself either rejecting some of the former in-home arrangements or being rejected by actors in such arrangements. An example of this is the ability to use the homes of friends and relatives only up to a certain point after the absence. To go beyond this would be to strain the already existing relationships between the relative or friend and the runner's parent(s). Also, to remain beyond this point in time with either a friend or a relative can prove to be a difficult thing to legitimatize. As the individual comes to realize this, the need to seek out new and more secure settings or territories quickly increases. Very often this takes the form of new friends, new locations, activities, challenges, etc. What once was an understanding between friends concerning a place to sleep now becomes an understanding between an individual and the YMCA for a weekly rental. What once was a problem of poor grades or poor attendance in school often shifts to no grades and no attendance. What once was a recreational excursion into the local shopping area or neighborhood night center becomes a definite excursion into the business community for the purpose of shoplifting. However, the exploration and finding of new persons to live or cope with, places to stay or things to do, in itself does not confirm the runaway designation. Such experiences contribute to the process but are not, in themselves, sufficient to provide automatic designation of a runaway label. What must be included, in addition to the above, is the confirmation by a social audience—an audience of persons who are seen daily, who are concerned with events and issues that are central to remaining away and who themselves may be concerned with the individual's survival in the near future. Not all persons encountered in this expanded social setting can contribute to such a definition process. Many respondents reported the need to "sort out," "feel around," and "be cool" with each new set of encounters and people. Numerous accounts were presented in which young persons demonstrated a "cautious optimism" about each new person. Many had learned that not all "new friends" are new friends! As was suggested by one male respondent:

> *The more you get beat. . .the more you know*
> *you don't want to never let that happen again.*
> *You will be careful!*

Thus, we do not only see a shift in concern from in-home to out-of-home concerns but also a shift in audience, which strains, interprets, reinforces and legitimizes the shift.

In some cases, young persons are not capable of

identifying or being identified with such audiences.

In this investigation, a number of reactions were identified in connection with failing to establish one's self as a runaway. The first response was withdrawal or absence again. This type of person simply decides to quit the location or scene and immediately does so. Since there was little "confirming" contact to begin with among others, this is rather easy to do. In this investigation, I encountered a number of young persons who appeared to do this by virtue of their not returning to the regular hangouts and by statements made by other young persons. Comments such as: "He had nothing going for him," and "He knows not to be back here," or blank-stares-as-expressions, indicated their was little feeling for the person. The second response was one of competition or challenge. Here, the individual was moving away to something more desirable, such as regular work or some routine illicit activity. Continued presence in this locale was viewed as stupid and not a desired course of behavior. In some cases, this might be looked upon as the direct opposite of the withdrawal response since the individual is viewed as having the skills but not choosing to use them -- at least not as a runner. The third type is what I have termed the "drifter or flounder" reaction because of the runners' general lack of knowing, or of being able to describe a routine location and social audience for themselves. These persons continually "flounder" around between crises and confidence, bouncing from situation to situation, or searching for people, places or things that they can be part of. Whether the individual searchers are successful or not — i.e., did or did not find an alternative residence, did or did not find new friends or a means of support — is most important in the process of how they come to see themselves (that one is or is not making it!). This realization serves as a basis upon which all future courses of action proceed. In that sense, these feelings are much like the realization of Goffman's (1961a) mental patients who feel they have been "deserted" by the outside world (p. 145). That is, the present situation of runaways begins to affect the way they feel about themselves as runaways, as persons trying to be runaways, as persons who are basing their opinion and behaviors upon what others think.

3. The Routinization Stage

Once an individual reaches the routinization stage, this marks the time when on-going consistent or regular relationships have been achieved by a person out of their home. In concrete terms, this means that individuals have gained such a degree of control over their daily routines that they can constructively anticipate problems, estimate success or failure and generally neutralize threats. To the degree that some who reach this stage often get temporarily locked into this lifestyle, we might view this as a confirmation or verification of the runaway status. Because individuals in the earlier stages have expanded and routinized their relationships in becoming runaways, they are now tied to other actors in the runaway scene. Activities, plans, problems, or critical events are held in common. The individual, at this point, can anticipate boundaries since he or she can now refer to the structure which sets boundaries. This structure is the activities of persons away from home, their problems, rules, expectations, fears, etc. Understanding this structure is what gives one the ability to identify and be identified by others in a similar situation. The individual who reaches this point typically is more confident about his/her position in life, views things in less immediate terms, and often stakes his/her future outside the home rather than inside it. To that extent, this final stage marks a transformation from the role of young-person-at-home to young-person-as-runaway, because individuals at this level can be more certain about their new role and role performance as runaway versus that of son or daughter in the home. This is particularly well evidenced by a statement cited earlier concerning school. An individual who had been away from home some time laughed at his current position. This stands in contrast to someone who takes such an issue as having recently left home with a degree of sobriety.

Stages and Interpretations of the Court

One indication that someone is shifting to the next stage of runaway behavior might be found in the different ways people come to interpret the court. Within this investigation, a number of young persons were identified as having been processed by the family court. In examining statements concerning the court, several patterns emerge. (1) The more

143

contact the young person has with the court, the more likely they are initially to view themselves as "in trouble" (especially in the unsettling stage). (2) However, as young persons move into later career stages, the court is interpreted with *decreasing significance* and there's an understanding that the court isn't going to do much.

In comparing family court descriptions made by young persons at the unsettling stage versus the routinization stage, these patterns are borne out, as shown in the examples on page 144..

As can be interpreted from these comments, young people are shaped by court but also, to a degree, by experiences within the court. What is at first a clear indication that the person is in trouble (because of the petition), later becomes an indication that everything is "under control." The young person who can estimate, and later predict, through past contact within the court, is the person in control. To be in control is, as one young person described it, "together." If you have been to court and little is done, you lose your fear.

Beyond perceptions of the court, the quality of language describing the court itself appears different from earlier to later stages. For example, derogatory statements describing the court, its personnel, judges, decisions, and confusion are readily made by those who have been to court. More was said and said with a very definite negative attitude as evidenced by this brief dialogue between myself and one young person.

Interviewer: "What do you mean by it (the court) doing nothing?"

Respondent: "That's it, *NOTHING* (with emphasis). Why does anybody expect anything to be done, what did anybody expect? I didn't do a fucking thing. Be *out*, that's it. That is what I did, and that stupid place keeps talking and talking and what not. Hey, a whole bunch of bullshit, for what? For bullshit."

Interviewer: "Well, then, why do you think the court bothers?"

Respondent: "It bothers, because the motherfuckers got nothing else to do. You know they get your

Unsettling   Versus

1. You know I didn't know what would happen (in the court). *Respondent No. 6 — Away 10 weeks*

2. I did not get any chance to talk. Like to let people understand all the problems. I would be talking to this guy who would take notes but there was never a judge over them. *Respondent No. 6 — Away 10 weeks*

3. We went to court several times. After like 3 times, we would get the same 'rundown'. . .we would shift. I wasn't going to school then so my mother thought it was important to keep going to court, but I didn't. I once told my sister that I was not going to show next time; she told me that I better or else they (court) would snatch my ass up! I thought about that and got really messed up behind that . . .ya know what they would do, Spafford stuff, so I made sure I was at the court. (Detention) *Respondent No. 19 — Away 7 weeks*

Routinization

1. They want me to go over to the court for not being home. We done all that shit before, you go down, they talk to you and that is it. No big thing. *Respondent No. 17 — Away 156 weeks*

2. I had it figured that soon as I got peeped for playing with drugs and since I was already out of the house, I was going to Spafford. No way, that ain't what jumped off! The judge is the thing. This was a different judge and she was okay. From now on I don't think you can figure what can happen to you, one day they will pop you, some days nothing. *Respondent No. 30 — Away 96 weeks*

3. The court, hey they don't do anything to you or for your mother but tell you that you need to listen and do what your mother says. You know like when you need to stay home. You see the judge don't know you cause he has to talk to a lot of kids. He tells us all the same thing. Sometimes they send you to a place that has counselors and programs to help you, but it's no help. You go a couple of times with the same people. After I go, my mother ain't mad at me no more, so I don't need to go to court. I don't know why I had to go to court, they can't do anything for you. It's only when my mother is mad. *Respondent No. 17 — Away 156 weeks*

4. Hey, that court shit, I would not take them serious. If I thought some real serious shit would happen I would. *Respondent No. 30 — Away 96 weeks*

problem, then they do their thing. . .which is nothing because these people can't give me nothing! After you get talked with, if you mess up "wham," they keep you up at the Bronx until they are ready to let you home, back and forth, back and forth."

Interviewer: "So, then, how do you see going to court?"

Respondent: "I don't see it, I never did see it, so I guess now I'm a little more sure it's bullshit!"

One explanation for why thinking about the family court shifts is that young people become better able to identify, interpret and estimate what is occurring around them. This is typified in the following quote:

I figured once I was first out I would get forced back in. But that was in the beginning. After I saw the same thing happen, I sort of got used to doing what I wanted to. These people don't know much; because they only see you once in a while and don't care about you anyway.

Respondent number 17

What is central to the above statement is that the experiences become familiar and thus routine. This is significant for several reasons, each central to a career model. (1) The experience is cumulative and each recurring official contact reinforces the feeling of "routine". (2) Young persons come to see how official social control agents act indifferently toward them. (3) Each new encounter brings the young person into an ever expanding network of young persons and adults who communicate new meanings. Taken together, these experiences serve to minimize the importance of the former "in-home" events and maximize the importance of out of home events. Further they serve to crystalize the status of young people out of their homes since such young persons become examples to other young people away from home (see previous chapter). This pattern extends into a number of daily episodes beyond the court to include family friends and skills. In Diagram I below, a number of these variables have been listed as they intersect with each stage of the suggested model.

DIAGRAM I
OVERVIEW OF RUNAWAY MODIFIERS BY RESPECTIVE STAGE

STAGE	MODIFIER					
	1 Family Contacts	2 Location of Residence	3 Perception of or About Court	4 Friendship Network	5 School Concerns	6 Skills
Unsettling stage	Emotion laden and defensive	Home based	Threatening	Home centered	Existent	Untested
Exploration Stage	Increasingly aggressive	Friend based	Inconsistent	In transition	Non-committal	Expanding
Routinization Stage	Infrequent or non-existent	Beyond friends	Indifferent	Transformed	Non-existent	A model for others

Ideal Patterns

Below is a set of "ideal patterns" suggested by both my data and the above discussion. Each is offered to provide some idea as to the distinct paths someone can travel in and out the runaway role. To the extent that this is a cumulative process, the reader is reminded that this is presented as an "ideal type" framework and does not in all cases ground itself in actual observation.

The Experimenter — Indifferent Individuals with the Unsettling Stage

This first stage can be seen as one point of entry for the out-of-home experience. In this instance, the individual has simply left home with little understanding about the implication for the future (i.e., they do not know how to anticipate court). Some young people do not anticipate problems at this point and view this absence and lack of a place to stay as incidental, and in no way a serious matter. For example, in some cases, young persons involved in a court-related matter choose to leave home to avoid prosecution. These persons have every intention of re-contacting home and do not see themselves as runaways.

The Novice — Indifferent Individuals within the Exploration State/Reevaluation

Beyond the unsettling stage, the indifferent person may begin to find the necessity to explore alternatives. This is often because a temporary absence becomes prolonged. Given the somewhat unexpected character of such events, one of three choices can be made: the individual can risk going home, begin to rely on friends or develop an individual routine or independence away from home.

The Independent — Indifferent Individuals within the Routine Stage

Once an individual chooses to travel the path away from home, yet does so via an individual or isolated route, we consider that person to be emancipated. This is an individual who has remained indifferent to the runaway theme, but has routinized most of the skills, resources, etc., which are necessary in remaining out of home. Such an individual does not establish himself viz-a-viz other actors, but instead has remained isolated. There is no social basis upon which this person can judge, or be judged, about his out-of-home experience. Such an individual is not a runaway (in this study) since the reflective basis and meanings upon which being a runaway are premised do not exist. In short, no social tie exists with a runaway scene, and in-home ties can be kept. Contacts, concerns and routines exist, independent of that group of persons who consider themselves runaways.

The Friend — Friendship Focused Individuals within the Unsettling Stage

If an individual actor, through his reevaluation, chooses to rely on friends, or the actor planned his absence by virtue of having friends, he would be included in this stage of development. In either case, the individual is still in the unsettling stage of the career. This is of particular interest in the case of the individual who, although originally indifferent toward the runaway scene, begins to see its relevance as an identity, given the inability to return home. In such instances, persons away from home begin to abandon isolation in favor of friends who might be supportive of their out-of-home status. However, despite the fact they have already been out of the home, their predicament remains unsettled. Likewise, for the person who decides to leave home through the assistance of friends, the first days can be described as uncertain or unsettling.

The Adventurer — Friendship Focused Individuals within the Exploration Stage

A person who is initially attracted to the idea of leaving home, and afterward finds it necessary to explore other means of survival, falls into this category. Such a person has typically discovered that friends and, in some cases, family have grown impatient and suspect, or are bored with the individual's routine. Upon reaching this stage, several realizations were reported by young people regarding survival. The first is that the position of friends often changes. It may be recalled that although friends themselves are often quite supportive of the individual who leaves home, parents are often unwilling to support or legitimate the absence of somebody else's child. The result is that friends often find themselves unable to provide further help to the absentee who needs to look elsewhere. This sort of development brings into focus the second point of expanding "social worlds." When and if the individual seeks out and finds supportive networks beyond friends or family, this usually means new contacts and friends. This represents the first instance of when someone might be considered to be moving toward a runaway status since the person is coming into objects, skills, concerns, language and other elements which, to this point, have been identified as part of the runaway scene. Unlike the exploration efforts of his indifferent counterpart, he has begun to make regular contacts with persons like himself — persons who can acknowledge his presence in this setting. Typically, these persons are more immersed in the day-to-day activity of the runaway scene. They can, therefore, advise, apply pressure or perhaps influence the person "exploring out" on behalf of returning home. We might look upon this as a semi-commitment to the daily runaway activity since individuals coming to accommodate such a lifestyle are, therefore, dependent upon each other in the scene. Recall the young woman who reported regular residence with a boyfriend until such time as he became engaged in illicit drug activity — such a person can be viewed as having "made ties" by virtue of directing her action and plans toward someone else, and they likewise reciprocate. However, such a person has yet to become committed or emotionally tied to this setting. It is to that point that I now turn.

The Survivor — Friendship Focused Individual within the Routinization Stage

Upon reaching a regular out-of-home routine — which implies contact with "others," friends, a regular means of survival and daily concerns — someone may be considered a runaway. Unlike any of the five previous types, this person is, for the most part, active on behalf of not returning, does not see home as an alternative, and has routinized and planned his activity around that not happening. Typically, such a person has resolved all of the unsettling problems identified in the first stage, and his person exploration has netted him a reasonable ability to survive away from home.

In the course of this investigation, such individuals were not identified as being independent or emancipated since a new dependence was being formed around the theme of using friends and contacts to remain away from home. In establishing a regular reliance on friends, typing one's plans to others, seeking new opinions and having them do likewise in reciprocal fashion, one is, in a sense, once again becoming dependent. The dependence becomes central to being able to plan activity and to avoid crises, etc. Without feeling some type of mutual dependence, actors cannot anticipate how each will respond to the other or how each will or can respond to another's needs.

The Street Person — Group Focused Individual in Unsettling Stage

This type of individual can be identified as devoting many of his or her energies toward a group of persons like himself upon immediately leaving home. Although in an unsettling stage, many of these young people have been out of their homes on earlier occasions. Having been away before, some people are very familiar with any runaway network which appears to be supportive. Much like his or her counterparts in earlier stages, events are unsettled. No clear delineation can be announced by the young person about how he will address the residual problems of home — such as school, the need to return and the anxiety about leaving. Despite the earlier absence, most individuals find it difficult to tackle these initial problems. However, unlike his or her counterparts, this individual can resort to friends or contacts with already existing definitions about the need to remain away from home. Often this is done via an involvement in Runaway Prevention Programs or Probation Intervention Programs. Both family and friends often recognize the uneasiness about remaining home *and*, in many cases, truly are indifferent about these problems. This group most probably has the greatest resemblance to "a throwaway child," to the degree that both seek attention, resources and support outside their home — well before they seek it through friends or other groups. A major reason for this is that the resources they bring to the runaway setting are more developed. A regular "pre-street identity" has formed and the young person uses it when things are going bad. Because this street culture places an existing value on the unconventional, we might view the individual as already familiar with some of

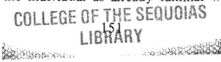

the techniques held as important by the group, the runaway program, etc. — prior to the actual absence. In a sure sense, they can be seen as young persons in search of supervision.

The Hustler — Group Focused Individuals within the Exploration Stage

Since individuals here typically move directly from being unsettled, they are characteristically better able to carry on exploration when compared with counterparts in earlier phases. They might be looked upon as similar to the state used by young people described by Irwin (1970) in his study of felon careers. Such young people are often the children of welfare families, public hospital services, subjects of earlier dependency or neglect petitions in the family court — and school problems. For such persons the choice is staying out of the home via the use of public agencies or through the use of somebody else. Respondents in this group talked about the "hustle" but few were certain about themselves — or certain about what to do. Those who felt their further exploration could "make life easier" often referred to training programs (CETA, etc.) which might "at once" provide an ability — keep them out of their home and finally make them independent, emancipated and somewhat conventional. To do this is to "make it" and to make it in or out of the home after having little is important to a young person. Often this stage is a choice between the hit or miss opportunities of the many public agencies which serve the poor or the fast hustle of the street. To that extent, illegal activities are relied upon when agencies do not appear attractive. Thus, if drug sales are the means of survival, they are used; if "low-grade" robberies are called for, they are engaged in. One individual in the group described himself as having power: A power to choose among alternatives.

The Runaway

This final group represents a routinization of a daily out-of-home lifestyle. Such young persons have not opted for emancipation; to that extent they may be seen as young persons who have been defined and define themselves as runaways.

That is, they have moved toward a more definite sense of "who one is," (Brissett, 1978). For these young people, the more obvious it becomes that they can remain away, the easier it becomes to concentrate on their newly acquired master status of runaway (Hughes, 1945). At this point, all the doubts become removed both in the eyes of peer group adults and youth advocates. The individual is, in fact, who (s)he presents himself to be. Absence from home provides the young person with a self conception and a dependable view of what and where they stand viz-a-viz others. Like in the case of the heavy drinker (Brissett, 1978), the acts of the "heavy drinker" and the heavy drinker's self conceptions are somewhat merged. . .

> . . .even though the excessive drinker is often seen negatively, he does stand as clearly an identifiable entity. In this sense, the individual who drinks excessively might not like who he is (self-evaluation), but he certainly knows who he is (self-conception).
>
> (Brissett; 1978:9)

CHAPTER VIII

CONCLUSIONS AND IMPLICATIONS

The major thrust of this investigation has placed emphasis upon the social and processual foundation that leads to becoming a runaway. Attention was focused on the everyday events which help shape both the runaway role and the young person's understanding of that role. Given this investigation's scope in the subjective dimension of children living out of their homes, several conclusions and observations are warranted.

First: Because of the wide range of behaviors identified among young people, it is imperative that distinctions be made between runaways and young people exhibiting other sorts of adolescent behavior. Leaving home is a dramatic event for young people, which requires the first-time management of everyday resources necessary for survival and safety. Because an adolescent may not be emotionally equipped to handle such a burden, and at the same time society may not allow them to, some of their activities take the form of non-conventional behavior. Parents, case workers and youth advocates must draw careful distinctions between those young people who are totally assertive about and committed to a new way of living, and young people who are delinquent, troubled or seeking help. Young people who are testing social boundaries on behalf of growing independent are distinctly different from young people who are bored, deprived or emotionally confused.

Second: Given the stages identified in this investigation, running away may best be understood as a process rather than a single event. No child automatically knows how to run away from home—runaway skills must be learned. This learning takes place through a series of social encounters experienced out of the home.

154

Third: In the initial stages of absence behavior, parents must recognize the critical role friends play in crystallizing the runaway experience. As a process, running away demands routine experimentation. A child's friends often are a critical support network for either approving or discouraging the continued absence. Parents must appreciate the degree to which children are dependent upon friends to provide peer support and reinforcement of the absence episode.

Fourth: Intervention on behalf of absence behavior must recognize the particular stages children "pass" through in the runaway process. Children leaving their homes report different needs at different points in the absence. The person reported away from home six months must be approached in ways different from those away only a short period of time. Our responses to absence must be multi-faceted and attentive to varied needs of children.

Fifth: Absence behavior is not necessarily a crisis or terminal event in a young person's life, nor does it always represent a total break with one's family. This investigation has highlighted and humanized both the positive and negative aspects of being a runaway. Unfortunately, it has too often been assumed that absence from home implies personal destruction rather than independence. This is ironic — especially in a nation which prides itself on both a past and present that emphasizes individualism. Various experiences reinforce the message of being an individual on a daily basis. In this country, from crib to casket, we are reminded of our God-given right to express ourselves freely, to be individual and to break away from the crowd. Both primary and secondary group sources in the form of family or peer and employers reward us for achievement which stands apart from all others.

However, not all aspects of the adolescent experience influence young people in the same way. In some cases, adolescents regularly fail to establish themselves or accomplish what Stone (1962) refers to as having "one's self located." Consequences of this include self doubts, insecurity and pain. Having one's self located as a runaway, at least in part, limits the problem of adolescence concerning "where identity fits in." In this sense, the identity of a runaway serves a positive purpose. I am not suggesting that it is absolutely wholesome for children to walk away from family;.

155

however, it is by no means destructive for some children — especially those with few social and economic options.

Sixth: We must distinguish between the social and legal definitions of runaways and the consequences of both perspectives. The primary intention of this book has been to clarify and expand the runaway definition based upon the subjective observations and experiences of the young people themselves. Earlier investigations have ignored the importance of subjective runaway accounts and instead stressed a narrower legal focus. This investigation has challenged the reliance on legal definitions alone by calling attention to the process through which one explores, learns and confirms for one's self the role and status of a runaway. In order to clearly define a runaway, this process requires the subjective reflection of children living the actual roles. The fact that so few young people in this investigation identified themselves as runaways or were labeled as such bears testimony to the lengthy duration and complicated process that creates runaways.

Both policymakers and official spokespeople would do well in recognizing that legal definitions do not always accurately depict the actions and philosophy of the young person away from home. Moreover, legal designations may actually compound the problem by misinterpreting a young person's behavior. Consequently, the use of legal definitions distorts the actual number of runaways that exist. Not all young people leave home in connection with problems and not all young people view themselves as runaways. Problems sometimes flow from contacts made after running away with both legal and advising groups. Many young people do not understand or want the continued involvement of agencies such as court since they generally prove to be ineffective and, in some cases, premature.

Seventh: Given the expanded focus provided for interpreting runaways, a broader range of services must be made available for children and parents managing the episode. Mobility has become the norm in American society. Children must be provided ample housing away from home while deciding what shape and form their new lifestyle will take. Young people and their parents must be given an opportunity to examine why neither party can live together. Similar to a trial separation in marriage, parents and children

156

must reserve judgment on the ill effects of absence, on behalf of better understanding of how it fits into an American life-style.

1. Introduction to Respondent: General purpose
2. Background Information
    a.   place of residence (formerly)
    b.   age
    c.   home setting, parents, brothers, sisters; how many?
    d.   problems in home, reason for leaving
    e.   court experience/petitions, etc.
    f.   number of times away in the past
    g.   how long have you remained away this time?
3. Present Situation
    a.   Why did you leave home this time?
    b.   Is this different from before?
    c.   Where are you living now?
    d.   How did you arrange this?
    e.   How long have you been there?
    f.   Do you plan to stay?
    g.   What about money; how do you get it?
    h.   Are there jobs, friends, welfare?
    i.   What do your friends do for money?
    j.   What sorts of "good" things have been happening to you?
    k.   What sorts of problems (crises) have you had in the past week?
    l.   Can you depend upon someone for help?
    m.   Who?
    n.   How did you get to find out about the "program"?
    o.   Have you used programs before?
    p.   Have your friends used them?
    q.   *At this point, I ask respondent to describe an average day. (Here I have been attempting to*

get examples of "good" situations and "problem" situations.)

4.   a.   How do you feel when you think about yourself now as compared with a month ago?
      b.   Is your situation better?
      c.   Is your situation worse?
      d.   What do you intend to do in the next month?

5.   a.   Do you want to go home?
      b.   Have you been home?
      c.   Do you think you will leave again?

APPENDIX II

DEMOGRAPHIC MASTER INDEX

The Demographic Master Index is presented as a point of clarity and as a summary device. This index represents an overview of who the respondent group is. This index is designed to match an identifying number to the respondent instead of his or her name. Listed next to each identifying number are prior absences. In previous pages these variables were examined individually, then examined in relationship to each other. In addition, reference may be made to the index when identifying specific quotes reported in the text.

DEMOGRAPHIC MASTER INDEX

Respondent	Age	Race	Sex	Length of Absence	Prior Absence
1	11	B	M	3 weeks	1
2	14	B	M	10 months	none
3	14	B	M	8 months	none
4	14	W	M	10 weeks	4
5	10	B	M	5 days - 1 week	none
6	11	SS	M	2 weeks	none
7	17	W	F	10 months	none
8	17	B	F	1 week	4
9	14	B	M	2 weeks	2
10	14	B	M	6 weeks	6
11	12	B	M	12 weeks	none
12	13	B	M	8 months	none
13	20	W	M	3 years, plus. . .	8
14	13	SS	M	7 weeks	5
15	15	W	M	10 months	none
16	16	W	F	24 weeks	8
17	14	SS	M	30 months	7
18	14	B	M	3 weeks	none
19	15	W	F	13 months	3
20	14	SS	M	13 months	5
21	14	B	M	14 months	5
22	15	SS	F	9 months	none
23	15	SS	M	10 weeks	3
24	18	W	F	10 months	none
25	18	W	F	12 weeks	none
26	15	SS	F	15 months	6
27	15	SS	M	14 months	4
28	15	SS	M	10 months	none
29	18	B	M	13 months	6
30	14	SS	M	20 months	10
31	15	B	M	16 months	2
32	16	SS	F	13 months	none
33	16	SS	F	10 weeks	2
34	16	B	M	10 weeks	none
35	15	W	M	8 months	none
36	16	B	M	15 months	none

BIBLIOGRAPHY

Ambrosino, L., "Youth in Trouble: Runaway." TODAY'S EDUCA-
TION, 1979, 70(9), pp. 26-28. *New York Publishings*

Antebi, R., "Some Characteristics of Mental Hospital Absconders."
BRITISH JOURNAL OF PSYCHIATRY, 1967, 113, pp. 1087-
1090.

Armbsky, R.E., "The Dolescent Crisis Team: An Experiment in Community Crises Intervention." Proceedings of the Annual Convention of the American Psychological Association, 1971, 6(2),
pp. 735-736.

Armstrong, C.P., "A Psychoneutrotic Reaction of Delinquent Boys and
Girls." JOURNAL OF ABNORMAL SOCIAL PSYCHOLOGY,
1937, 32(3-4), pp. 329-342.

_____, 660 RUNAWAY BOYS: WHY BOYS DESERT THEIR
HOMES. Boston: Badger, 1932.

Ball, Donald, "An Abortion Clinic Ethnography." SOCIAL PROB-
LEMS, 1966, XIV, No. 3, pp. 293-301.

Balser, B.H., "A Behavior Problem--Runaways." PSYCHIATRIC
QUARTERLY, 1939, 13, pp. 539-557.

Banouhl, M., OFFICE OF YOUTH DEVELOPMENT NEWSLETTER,
March, 1975.

Becker, Howard, "Constructive Typology in the Social Sciences."
AMERICAN SOCIOLOGICAL REVIEW, 1940, 5, pp. 40-5.

_____, "Field Methods and Techniques: A Note on Interviewing
Tactics." HUMAN ORGANIZATION, 1954, 12, pp. 31-2.

_____, "Notes on the Concept of Commitment." AMERICAN
JOURNAL OF SOCIOLOGY, 1960, 66, pp. 32-40.

_____, OUTSIDERS: STUDIES IN THE SOCIOLOGY OF DE-
VIANCE. 1963, New York: The Free Press.

_____, SOCIOLOGICAL WORK: METHOD AND SUBSTANCE.
Aldin Publishing Company, 1970, Chicago.

_____ and Carper, Jr., "The Elements of Identification with an
Occupation." AMERICAN SOCIOLOGICAL REVIEW, 1956a,
22, pp. 341-348.

_____, " The Development of Identification with an Occupation." AMERICAN JOURNAL OF SOCIOLOGY, 1956b, 61, pp. 289-298.

_____ and Strauss, A., "Careers, Personality and Adult Socialization." AMERICAN JOURNAL OF SOCIOLOGY, 1956, 62, pp. 253-263.

_____, Geer, B., Hughes, E.C. and Strauss, A.L. (eds.), BOYS IN WHITE. University of Chicago Press, Chicago, 1961.

_____, Geer, B., Riesman, D. and Weiss, R. S. (eds.) INSTITUTIONS AND THE PERSON, Chicago: Aldine Publishing Company, 1968a.

_____, Gerr, B. and Hughes, E.C., MAKING THE GRADE: THE ACADEMIC SIDE OF COLLEGE LIFE. John Wiley & Sons, Inc., 1968b.

Beggs, L. HUCKLEBERRY'S FOR RUNAWAYS. New York: Ballantine Books, 1969.

Blankenship, Ralph L., "Organizational Careers." SOCIOLOGICAL QUARTERLY, 14:88-98, 1973.

Blaylock, B., "Diogenes House Helps Troubled." SACRAMENTO BEE, July 22, 1975.

Blumberg, Abraham, CRIMINAL JUSTICE. Quadrangle Books, Inc., Chicago, IL., 1967.

Blumer, H., "Psychological Import of the Human Group," in Muzafer Sheriff and M. O. Wilson (eds.), GROUP RELATIONS AT THE CROSSROADS. NY: Harper & Brothers, 1953, pp. 185-202.

_____, "Society as Symbolic Interaction," in Arnold M. Rose (ed.), HUMAN BEHAVIOR AND SOCIAL PROCESSES. Boston: Houghton Mifflin Company, 1962, pp. 179-192.

_____, "Sociological Implications of the Thought of George Herbert Mead." AMERICAN JOURNAL OF SOCIOLOGY, 1966, 71:535-548.

_____, SYMBOLIC INTERACTIONISM: PERSPECTIVE AND METHOD. Englewood Cliffs, New Jersey: Prentice-Hall, Inc., 1969.

Bock, R.D. GOT ME ON THE RUN: A STUDY OF RUNAWAYS. Boston, Mass., 1973.

Bracey, Dorothy, TEENAGE PROSTITUTION IN NEW YORK CITY. New York State Office of Crime Control Planning, Midtown Enforcement Project, 1977.

Brenner, J., "A Free Clinic for Street People: Medical Care without a Hassle," NEW YORK TIMES MAGAZINE, October 11, 1972.

Brennen, T., et al., FINAL REPORT: THE INCIDENCE AND NA-

TURE OF RUNAWAY BEHAVIOR, for Department of Health, Education and Welfare, 1975.

Brooks, P., "They Can Go Home Again," McCALLS, June 1972.

_____, "360 Boys and Girls, 11-17, Counseling Follow-Ups," San Diego, California, 1976.

Brown, C., MANCHILD IN THE PROMISED LAND, New York: Mac millan, 1965.

Brisset, D., "Toward an American Understanding of Heavy Drinking," PACIFIC SOCIOLOGICAL REVIEW, Vol. 21, Number 1, January, 1978, pp. 3-21.

Byrne, N., "Socio-temporal Consideration of Everyday Life Suggested by an Empirical Study of the Bar Milieu," URBAN LIFE, Vol. 6, No. 4, 1978.

Bruyn, S.T., THE HUMAN PERSPECTIVE IN SOCIOLOGY: THE METHODOLOGY OF PARTICIPANT OBSERVATION. Englewood Cliffs, New Jersey: Prentice-Hall, Inc., 1966.

Cambareri, J. D., Sagers, P. S. & Tatton, D. F., "The AWOL from a Juvenile Institution." CRIME AND DELINQUENCY, 1960, 6(4), pp. 275-278.

Campbell, D. L., "Three Runaway Children." M.A.Thesis, Richmond School of Social Work, College of William and Mary, Richmond Professional Institute, 1947.

Canadian Council on Social Development, TRANSIENT YOUTH. 55 Parkdale, Ottawa 3, February, 1970.

Cavan, Sherri, "Interaction in Home Territories," BERKLEY JOURNAL OF SOCIOLOGY, 1963.

_____, LIQUOR LICENSE: AN ETHNOGRAPHY OF BAR BEHAVIOR. Chicago, Aldine, 1966.

Chapan, C., AMERICA'S RUNAWAY. New York: Wm. Morrow Press, 1976.

Charon, Joel M., SYMBOLIC INTERACTIONISM. Prentice-Hall, Englewood Cliffs, NJ, 1979.

Cicourel, Aaron V., THE SOCIAL ORGANIZATION OF JUVENILE JUSTICE. NY: John Wiley, 1968.

Clarke, R.V.G., "Absconding and Adjustment to the Training Schools." BRITISH JOURNAL OF CRIMINOLOGY, 1968, 8(3), pp. 285-295.

_____, "Approved School Absconders and Corporal Punishment," BRITISH JOURNAL OF CRIMINOLOGY. 1966, 6(1), pp. 364-375.

_____, "Season and Other Environmental Aspects of Absconding by Approved School Boys." BRITISH JOURNAL OF CRIMI-

NOLOGY, 1967, 7(2), pp. 195-206.

Clines, F. K., "About New York: In the Bario, A Hot Line That Cares." NEW YORK TIMES, May 25, 1978.

Cogdill, O., "Runaways: The Ultimate Trip." CLARION-LEDGER, Jackson, Mississippi, March 11, 1975.

Coleman, R., "Racial Differences in Runaways." PSYCHOLOGICAL REPORTS, 1968, 22(1), pp. 321-322.

Community Health and Welfare Council of Hennepin County, Inc., RUNAWAY YOUTH IN MINNEAPOLIS, Minneapolis, MN, 1971.

_____, FOLLOW-UP STUDY OF RUNAWAY YOUTH SERVED BY THE BRIDGE. Minneapolis, MN, 1972.

Cressey, Donald and Sutherland, Edwin, (eds.), CRIMINOLOGY, J.B. Lippincott, New York, 1970.

"Crisis Center," Hinds County, Mississippi. Hary Hughes, Director; Seeking funds to keep center open, 1976.

"Criticism and Crowding Crumble Image of Center for Runaways," Runaway House, 2117 Monroe, Memphis, TN, 1976.

Cryer, B., "Dear Cindy, We miss you. . .please call." ST. PETERSBURG (FLA.) TIMES, April 13, 1975.

Crystal, D. & Gold, I.H., "A Social Work Mission to Hippieland." CHILDREN, 1969, 16(1), pp. 28-32.

Dalton, M., "Informal Factors in Career Achievement." AMERICAN JOURNAL OF SOCIOLOGY, 1951, 56, pp. 407-415.

_____, MEN WHO MANAGE. NY: John Wiley & Sons, 1959.
_____, "Preconceptions and Methods in Men Who Manage," in Philip E. Mammond (ed.), SOCIOLOGISTS AT WORK. NY: Anchor Books, 1967.

Dandurand, Y., "Training School Wards Running Away from After-care Placement," CANADIAN JOURNAL OF CRIMINOLOGY AND CORRECTION, 17(4), October 1975, pp. 292-306.

David, L., "Are you runaway prone? Teenage girl runaways," SEVEN-TEEN, April 19, pp. 146-147.

Davis, F., "Deviance Disavowal: The Management of Strained Inter-action by the Visibly Handicapped." SOCIAL PROBLEMS, 1961, 9, pp. 120-132.

_____, PASSAGE THROUGH CRISIS: POLIO VICTIMS AND THEIR FAMILIES. Bobbs-Merrill.

Davis, Kenneth Culp, DISCRETIONARY JUSTICE: A PRELIMINARY INQUIRY, University of Indiana, 1969.

Denzin, Norman, THE RESEARCH ACT. Chicago: Aldine Publishing Company, 1970.

Douglas, J. D., RESEARCH ON DEVIANCE. Random House, New York, 1972.

_____, DEVIANCE AND IDENTITY, Prentice Hall, 1969.

Dreitzel, Haas, Peter, RECENT SOCIOLOGY, NO. 2: PATTERNS OF COMMUNICATIVE BEHAVIOR, MacMillan Co., New York, 1970.

Dumford, Franklyn, National Survey of Youth Runaways, for Office of Youth Development, Behavioral Research Corp., Washington, D.C., 1975.

Eisner, E.A., "Relationship Formed by Sexually Delinquent Adolescent Girls." AMERICAN JOURNAL OF ORTHOPSYCHIATRY, 1945, 15(2), pp. 301-308.

Emerson, Joan, JUDGING DELINQUENTS, CONTEXT AND PROCESS IN THE JUVENILE COURT, 1969.

English, C. J., "Leaving Home: A Typology of Runaways," SOCIETY, July-August, 1973, pp. 22-4.

Farrington, Donald S., "Observations on Runaway Children from a Residential Setting." CHILD WELFARE, 1963, pp. 286-291.

Feinberg, M. R., "Why Do Executives' Children Runaway?" interview, ed. by S. Margetta, DUNS, January 1968, pp. 40-2.

Fields, Sidney, "The Runaway Season Is On," NEW YORK DAILY NEWS, July 5, 1978.

_____, "Where Do Runaways Go?", NEW YORK DAILY NEWS, July 6, 1978.

Flanigan, B., "Black Runaways Increase," (Detroit) MICHIGAN CHRONICAL, July 26, 1975.

Forer, L., NO ONE WILL LISTEN, Universal Library, New York, 1970.

Foster, R. M., "Intrapsychic and Environment Factors in Running Away From Home," AMERICAN JOURNAL ORTHOPSYCHIATRY, 1962, pp. 486-491.

Frankel, Marvin, CRIMINAL SENTENCES, Hill and Wang, NY, 1972.

Friedson, E., PROFESSION OF MEDICINE, Dodd Mean, NY, 1970.

Gans, H., "The Participant-Observer as a Human Being; Observations on the Personal Aspects of Field Work." Howard S. Becker, Blanche Geer, David Riesman and Robert Weiss (eds.), INSTITUTIONS AND THE PERSON. Chicago: Aldine Publishing Company, pp. 300-317, 1968.

Garfinkel, H., STUDIES IN ETHNOMETHODOLOGY. Englewood Cliffs, NJ: Prentice-Hall, Inc., 1967.

"Gentle Marcy: A shattering tale; runaway to hippieland," NEWSWEEK, October 30, 1976, pp. 88-9.

Gerson, Ehliu, "On Quality of LIfe," ASR, Vol. 445, 1976, pp. 793-807.

166

Glaser, Barney G. (ed.), ORGANIZATIONAL CAREERS. Chicago: Aldine Publishing Company, 1968.

_____ and Strauss, A., THE DISCOVERY OF GROUNDED THEORY. Chicago, Aldine Publishing Company, 1968.

_____, TIME FOR DYING. Chicago: Aldine, 1968.

_____, STATUS PASSAGE. Chicago: Aldine-Atherton Publishing Company, 1971.

Glick, Selma; Robinson, Jane. N.Y.C. RUNAWAYS, New York City Youth Board, 1976.

Goffman, Erving. ASYLUMS. NY: Anchor Books, 1961a.

_____, THE PRESENTATION OF SELF IN EVERYDAY LIFE. NY: Anchor Books, 1959.

_____, ENCOUNTERS. Indianapolis: The Bobbs-Merrill Company, Inc., 1961b.

_____, BEHAVIOR IN PUBLIC PLACES. NY: The Free Press, 1963.

_____, INTERACTION RITUAL. NY: Anchor Books, 1967.

_____, "The Neglected Situation," in Howard S. Becker, Blanche Geer, David Riesman, and Robert Weiss, (eds.), INSTITUTION AND THE PERSON. Chicago: Aldine Publishing Company, 1968, pp. 295-299.

_____, "On Face Work," PSYCHIATRY, 18:1955, pp. 213-231.

Goldberg, M., "Runaway Americans," MENTAL HYGIENE. Winter, 1972.

Gordon, James, "The Washington, D.C. Runaway House," JOURNAL OF COMMUNITY PSYCHOLOGY, January 1975, pp. 68-80.

Greene, N. B. & Esselstyne, T. C., "The Beyond Control Girl," JUVENILE JUSTICE, 1972, 23(3), pp. 13-19.

Grisso, J. Thomas, "Conflict about release: Environmental and personal conditions among institutionalized delinquents," JOURNAL OF COMMUNITY PSYCHOLOGY, October 1975, pp. 396-99.

Gubrium, J.F., "Death Worlds in a Nursing Home," URBAN LIFE, Vol. 4, No. 3, October 1975, pp. 317-339.

Gurasekara, M.G.S., "The Problem of Absconding in Boys Approved Schools in England and Wales," BRITISH JOURNAL OF CRIMINOLOGY, 1963, 4(2), pp. 145-151.

Gussow, D., "Parents Tell Their Story," TALLAHASSEE (FLA.) DEMOCRAT, March 2, 1975.

Guthrie, A., Jr. and Howell, M., "Mobile medical care for alienated youths," JOURNAL PED., 1972, pp. 1025-1033.

Hackman, Theordore G., Homeless Youth in NYC: A field Study. Community Service Society, NYC., 1977.

Hall, Ozwald, "The Stages of a Medical Career, AJS, No. 53, March 1949, pp. 327-37.

Harrison, Saul L., Hess, John H. and Zrull, J. P., "Paranoid reactions in children," JOURNAL OF AMERICAN ACAD. CHILD PSY-CHIATRY, 1963, pp. 677-692.

Hawkins, R., Tiedeman, G., THE CREATION OF DEVIANCE. Charles E. Merrill Publishing Co., Columbus, OH, 1975.

Hildebrand, J.A., "Why Runaways Leave Home," JOURNAL OF CRIMINAL LAW, CRIMINOLOGY AND POLICE SCIENCE, 1963.

Hirschi, T., CAUSES OF DELINQUENCY. Berkeley, CA: University of California Press, 1969.

Homer, L.E., "community-based resource for runaway girls," SOCIAL CASEWORK, October 1973, pp. 473-79.

Howell, M. C., "Reminiscences of runaway adolescents," AMERICAN JOURNAL ORTHOPSYCHIATRY, 1973, pp. 840-53.

Hughes, Everett C., "Dilemmas and Contradictions of Status," AJS, March, 1945, pp. 353-359.

Irwin, J., THE FELON. Prentice Hall, 1970.

Jacobs, J., DEVIANCE: FIELD STUDIES AND SELF DISCLOSURES. National Press Books, Palo Alto, California, 1974.

Jenkins, R.L., "The runaway reaction," AMERICAN JOURNAL OF PSYCHIATRY, August 1971, pp. 168-173.

_____ and Stahle, Galen, "The runaway reaction: A case study," JOURNAL OF AMERICAN ACADEMY CHILD PSYCHIATRY. April 1972, pp. 294-313.

Jones, P. M., "Teenage Wanderers: Huckleberry House Shelter in San Francisco," SENIOR SCHOLASTIC, February 1974, pp. 6-13.

Katz, Michale, B., CLASS BUREAUCRACY AND SCHOOLS. Praeger Publishers, NY, 1971.

Katz, Sanford N., THE YOUNGEST MINORITY: LAWYERS IN DE-FENSE OF CHILDREN. American Bar Association, ABA Press, 1974.

Keifer, E., "Please. . .ask my mother if I can come home. Operation Peace of mind," GOOD HOUSEKEEPING, Sept. 1976.

Klonski, James Mendelsohn, THE POLITICS OF LOCAL JUSTICE. Little, Brown and Company, 1970.

Komisar, Lucy, DOWN AND OUT IN THE USA, 1977.

Larsen, R., "Runaways," PTA MAGAZINE, November 1972, pp. 26-32.

Lee, McClung, Alfred, PRINCIPLES OF SOCIOLOGY, Barnes J. Noble Books, 1969, pp. 1-50.

Lemert, E.M., SOCIAL PATHOLOGY. New York: McGraw-Hill, 1951.

Lerner, S., "The Judson House Quad: Runaways Cum Laude," VILLAGE VOICE, Dec. 5, 1968, p. 5.

Leventhal, T., "Control problems in runaway children," AMA & GENERAL PSYCHIATRY, 1963, pp. 122-128.

Levinson, B. and Mezei, H., "Self-concepts and ideal self-concepts of runaway youths: Counseling Implications," PSYCHOLOGICAL REPORTS, 1970, pp. 871-874.

Lewis, O., THE CHILDREN OF SANCHEZ. New York: Random House, 1961.

Libertoff, Kenneth, RUNAWAY CHILDREN AND SOCIAL NETWORK INTERACTION. U. S. Government Printing Office, 1976.

Liebow, E., TALLY'S CORNER. Boston: Little, Brown & Company, 1967.

Loeb, Margaret, "The Good Shepherd of 42nd Street," THE DAILY NEWS, April 3, 1978.

Lofland, John, "Interactionist Imagery and Analytic Interruptus," in Tamotsu Shibutani (ed.), HUMAN NATURE AND COLLECTIVE BEHAVIOR. Englewood Cliffs, NJ: Prentice-Hall, Inc., 1970, pp. 35-45.

_____, ANALYZING SOCIAL SETTINGS. Belmont, CA: Wadsworth Publishing Company, Inc., 1971.

Luckenbill, David F., Best, Joel, "Careers in Deviance and Responsibility: The Analogy's Limitations, SOCIAL PROBLEMS, Vol. 29, 2, 1981.

Lyman, S.M. and Scott, M. B., "Territoriality: A Neglected Sociological Dimension," SOCIAL PROBLEM, 1967, 15, pp. 236-249.

Mack, Julian W., "The Chancery Procedure in the Juvenile Court in Jane Addams, ed., THE CHILD, THE CLINIC AND THE COURT, p. 315.

Maines, D. R., "Social Organization and Social Structure in Symbolic Interactionist Thought," ANNUAL REVIEW SOCIOLOGY, 1977, pp. 3, 235-59.

MacLeod, C., "Street Girls of the '70's," NATION, April 30, 1974, pp. 386-8.

Manis, J. G., and Meltzer, B. (eds.), SYMBOLIC INTERACTION: A READER IN SOCIAL PSYCHOLOGY. Boston: Allyn and Bacon, Inc., 1972.

Matza, David, DELINQUENT AND DRIFT. John Wiley & Sons, Inc., New York, 1964.

169

Mann, Corame, Richey. "Legal and Judicial Battles Affecting Runa-
    ways," in Nye, Ivan F., Edelbrook, "Runaways," JOURNAL OF
    FAMILY ISSUES, Vol. 1, No. 2, June 1980.

McCall, G. J. & Simmons, J. L., IDENTITIES AND INTERACTION.
    NY: The Free Press, 1966.

McNeill, D., "Parents and Runaways. Writing a New Contract," VIL-
    LAGE VOICE, Dec. 14, 1967, p. 1.

_____, "Police and Runaways. The Policies of Garbese," VILLAGE
    VOICE, Dec. 7, 1967, p. 3.

McReady, George, "Locating Runaways." JOURNAL OF POLICE
    SCIENCE, Fall, 1978.

Mead, G. H., MIND, SELF AND SOCIETY. Chicago: University of
    Chicago Press, 1934.

Minutes of Subcommittee on Detention and Placement Facilities for
    Children in New York City, April 29, 1971.

Minutes of the Community Council of Greater New York, Re: Run-
    aways in New York City, February 9, 1978, Committee of
    Community Social Researchers, February 9, 1978.

Morgan, Tom, "Little Ladies of the Night: Runaways in New York,"
    NEW YORK TIMES MAGAZINE, Nov. 16, 1975, pp. 34-8.

Morgan, Edmund, THE PURITAN FAMILY. Harper & Row, New
    York, 1966.

Nye, Ivan F.; Edelbrook, Craig. "Runaways" JOURNAL OF FAMILY
    ISSUES, Vol. 1, No. 2, June, 1980.

Newman, Donald, "Pleading Guilty for Considerations: A study of
    Bargain Justice," THE JOURNAL OF CRIMINAL LAW, CRIM-
    INOLOGY AND POLICE SCIENCE, 46 March-April 1956, pp.
    780-790.

Palenski, Joseph, "Alternatives to Secure Detention in N.Y.C.," May-
    or's Office of Criminal Justice Coordinator, N.Y.C., 1972.

_____, "Socio-Economic Levels and the Rehabilitation of Drug
    Addicts," Unpub. Masters Thesis, Hunter College, N.Y.C., 1972.

Paul, "Etiology and Runaways," JOURNAL OF CRIMINAL LAW,
    CRIMINOLOGY AND POLICE SCIENCE, March-April 1954.

Peters, W., "Riddle of Teenage Runaways," GOOD HOUSEKEEPING
    June 1968, pp. 88-89.

Platt, Anthony M., THE CHILD SAVERS. The University of Chicago
    Press, Chicago, 1969.

Polsky, Ned, HUSTLERS, BEATS AND OTHERS. Chicago: Aldine,
    1967.

"Project Place: Year-end Report," Boston, MA, 1971.

Raphael, Maryanne, RUNAWAYS: AMERICA'S LOST YOUTH. NY:

Drake Publications, 1974. *P9 /25*

Reiss, Albert J., Jr., "Sex Offenses: The Marginal Status of the Adolescent," LAW AND CONTEMPORARY PROBLEMS, 1976.

Remsberg, C. & Remsberg, B., (eds.) "How Teen Runaways Get Help; Huckleberry House, San Francisco," SEVENTEEN, June 1972, pp. 122-123.

_____, "What Happens To Teen Runaways; Interviews With Two Runaway Girls," SEVENTEEN, June 1976, pp. 114-115.

Richardson, Stephan, Dohrenwend, Barbara, and Klein, David, INTERVIEWING: ITS FORM AND FUNCTIONS. NY, 1965.

Ringold, E. S., "Why They Run Away From Home," NEW YORK TIMES MAGAZINE, May 1, 1964, pp. 63-64.

Robbins, I. and Robbins, Jr., "Nice Girls Who Run Away," McCALL'S November 1966, pp. 114-115.

Robey, A., "The Runaway Girl," in FAMILY DYNAMICS AND FEMALE SEXUAL DELINQUENCY. Palo Alto, CA: Science and Behavior Books, 1969.

Robins, Lee N. and O'Neil, Patricia, "The Adult Prognosis for Runaway Children." AMERICAN JOURNAL ORTHOPSYCHIATRY, 1959, pp. 752-761.

Rose, Annelies Argelander, "The Homes of Homesick Girls," JOURNAL OF CHILD PSYCHIATRY, 1948, pp. 181-189.

Rose, Arnold M., "A Systematic Summary of Symbolic Interaction Theory," in Arnold M. Rose (ed.), HUMAN BEHAVIOR AND SOCIAL PROCESSES, Boston: Houghton-Mifflin Co., 1962, pp. 3-19.

Rosenhum, Marvin, "Returning Home," JOURNAL OF CHILD PSYCHIATRY, 1958.

Roth, Julius A., THE TREATMENT OF TUBERCULOSIS AS A BARGAINING PROCESS. Boston: Houghton-Mifflin Co., 1961, pp. 575-588.

Roy, Donald, "The STudy of Southern Labor Union Organizing," in Robert W. Habenstein (ed.), PATHWAYS TO DATA. Chicago: Aldine Publishing Co., 1970, pp. 216-244.

Rumer, Morris, "Perception of Runaways," JOURNAL OF CHILD PSYCHIATRY, March, 1958.

"Runaway Children," U.S.NEWS & WORLD REPORT, April 24, 1972, pp. 38-42.

"Runaway Kids," LIFE, Nov. 3, 1967, pp. 18-29.

"Runaways: A Million Bad Trips, How YOuth Agencies Try To Help," NEWSWEEK, October 26, 1970, pp. 67-68.

"Runaways: A National Problem," TIME, Aug. 27, 1973, p. 57.

"Runaways: A Non-Jucicial Approach," NEW YORK UNIVERSITY
LAW REVIEW, 1974.

"Runaways: A Non-suicidal Approach," NEW YORK UNIVERSITY
LAW REVIEW, 1974, pp. 110-130.

"Runaways: A Rising U. S. Worry," U.S. NEWS AND WORLD RE-
PORT, Sept. 3, 1973, p. 34.

"Runaways: Teenagers Who Run Away To The Hippies," TIME,
Sept. 15, 1967, p. 16.

"Running Away: Hard Way Out For Troubled Teens," CHICAGO
(IL) TRIBUNE, June 11, 1975.

Saling, A., "Refuge For Runaway Teenagers. Seattle's Ark Project,"
PARENTS MAGAZINE, Nov. 1974, pp. 76-77.

San Giovanni, Lucinda, EX-NUNS: A STUDY IN EMERGENT ROLE,
Passace, Norwood, New Jersey, Ablex, 1978.

Schatman, Leonard; Strauss, Anselm, FIELD STRATEGIES FOR A
NATURAL SOCIOLOGY, Prentice-Hall, 1973.

Schur, Edwin M., CRIMES WITHOUT VICTIMS. Englewood Cliffs,
New Jersey: Prentice-Hall, 1965.

_____, "Reactions to Deviance: A Critical Assessment," AMER-
ICAN JOURNAL OF SOCIOLOGY, 75 (Nov.): 1969, pp.
309-322.

_____, LABELING DEVIANT BEHAVIOR: ITS SOCIOLOGICAL
IMPLICATIONS. New York: Harper & Row, 1971.

_____, "The Concept of Secondary Deviation: Its Theoretical
Significance and Empirical Elusiveness," unpublished manu-
script, 1974.

Scott, Marvin B., THE RACING GAME. Chicago: Aldine Publishing
Company, 1968.

Shaynor, R. L., "From A Hippie's Soule: WNEW's A Child Again
broadcast." SATURDAY REVIEW, December 16, 1967,
p. 46.

Sidman, L., "The Massachusetts Stubborn Child Law: Law and Order
In The Home," FAMILY LAW QUARTERLY, 1972, pp.
33-57.

Silverman, Bill, "Why Do Children Run Away?" PARENTS MAGA-
ZINE, August 1963.

Simonsen, G. and Gordon, Marshall III, JUVENILE JUSTICE IN
AMERICA, Glencoe Publishing Company, Encino, California, 1979.

Slagle, Alton, "Thrown Away New York's Lost Children," NEW
YORK DAILY NEWS, Sunday, March 13, 1977.

Smith, Alexander and Pollack, Harriet, CRIME AND JUSTICE IN

MASS SOCIETY. Xerox Corp., 1972.

Savitz, Leonard, D.; Johnston, Norman, CRIME IN SOCIETY. John Wiley & Sons, New York, 1978.

Staub, Hugo, "A Runaway From Home," PSYCHOANALITIC QUARTERLY, 1943, pp. 1-22.

Stebbins, Robert A., "Career: The Subjective Approach," THE SOCIOLOGICAL QUARTERLY, 11:32:49

_____, COMMITMENT TO DEVIANCE, Glenwood, Westport, Conneticut.

Steffens, Lincoln, THE SHAME OF THE CITIES, NY: McClure-Phillips, 1904.

Stierlin, Helen, "A Family Perspective on Adolescent Runaways," Arch. GENERAL PSYCHIATRY, July 1973, pp. 56-62.

_____, SEPARATING PARENTS AND ADOLESCENTS: A PERSPECTIVE ON RUNNING AWAY, SCHIZOPHRENIA AND WAYWARDNESS. New York: Quadrangle, NY Times Book, 1974.

Stone, Gregory P. "Appearance and the Self," in Arnold M. Rose, HUMAN BEHAVIOR AND SOCIAL PROCESSES, Boston: Houghton-Mifflin Co., 1962, pp. 86-118.

_____ and Faberman, Harvey A. (eds.), SOCIAL PSYCHOLOGY THROUGH SYMBOLIC INTERACTION. Waltham, MA: Xerox College Publishing, 1970.

Strauss, Anselm, MIRRORS AND MASKS, THE SEARCH FOR IDENTITY. Free Press, 1959.

Sudnow, David, PASSING ON: THE SOCIAL ORGANIZATION OF DYING. Englewood Cliffs, NJ: Prentice Hall, Inc., 1967.

Sutherland, Edwin; Cressey, Donald, CRIMINOLOGY, ed., J. B. Lippincott, New York, 1970.

Testimony of Jerome M. Becker, Chairman, N.Y.C. Youth Board Before the New York State Assembly Committee on Child Care Concerning Runaways and Juvenile Prostitution, Nov. 30, 1976.

Thomas, W.I., THE UNADJUSTED GIRL. Boston: Little, Brown & Co., 1923.

Travisano, Richard V., Alternation and Conversion as Qualitatively Different Transformations, in Stone and Faberman, SOCIAL PSYCHOLOGY THROUGH SYMBOLIC INTERACTION, Xerox Corp., 1970, pp. 394-606.

Tsubouchi, K. and Jenkins, R., "Three Types of Delinquents: Their Performance on MMPI and PCR," JOURNAL CLINICAL PSYCHOLOGY, 1969, pp. 353-358.

Tunley, R., "If You're Thinking of Running Away," SEVENTEEN,

February 1968, pp. 138-139.

Turner, Ralph H., "Sponsored and Contest Mobility in the School System," AMERICAN SOCIOLOGICAL REVIEW, 25:855-867, 1960.

_____, "Role-Taking: Process Versus Conformity," in Arnold M. Rose (ed.), HUMAN BEHAVIOR AND SOCIAL PROCESSES, Boston: Houghton-Mifflin Co., 1962, pp. 20-40.

U. S. Dept. of Justice, Federal Bureau of Investigation. UNIFORM CRIME REPORT, 1-68-1971. Washington, D.C.: U. S. Government Printing Office, 1972.

Van Houten, L., Office of Youth Development, YOUTH ALTERNATIVES NEWSLETTER, April 1976, p. 32.

Ventura, Rafael, "Ways to Assist Homeless Youths Addressed by Groups of Experts." JOHN JAY JOURNALIST, May 23, 1978, p. 6.

Walker, D., "Runaway Youth: An Annotated Bibliography and Brief Literature Overview," for Department of Health, Education and Welfare, 1974.

Waller, Willard, "The Definition of the Situation," in Gregory P. Stone and Harvey A. Faberman (eds.) SOCIAL PSYCHOLOGY THROUGH SYMBOLIC INTERACTION, Waltham, MA: 1974.

Welch, M.S., "New Runaways," McCALL'S, November, 1974.

Wells, Gary, "What Moves a Child to Leave Home," (Duval County) FLORIDA TIMES WEEKLY, April 21, 1975.

"We've Been Asked About Hotlines for Runaways," U.S. NEWS & WORLD REPORT, February 24, 1975, p. 34.

"What To Do If Your Child Runs Away," BUSINESS WEEK, January 27, 1975, pp. 91-92.

Whythe, William F., STREET CORNER SOCIETY, 11th edition, University of Chicago Press, 1967.

Wilson, Thomas, "Running Away," SOCIAL CASEWORK, 1975, pp. 51-60.

Youcha, G., "Running Away, All the Way Home," PARENTS MAGAZINE, May 1973, pp. 48-49.

Zastron, C. and Navarre, R., "Help For Runaways and Their Parents," SOCIAL CASEWORK, 1975, pp. 74-78.

Zimmerman, Donald, "Ethnomethodology and the Problem of Order: Comment on Denzin," in Jack Douglas (ed.), UNDERSTANDING EVERYDAY LIFE. Chicago: Aldine, 1970.

174

ABOUT THE AUTHOR

Dr. Palenski is currently an Assistant Professor of Sociology and Criminal Justice at Seton Hall University. He has served as the former Director of Research for the New York City Youth Board, and as a staff associate to a number of regional and national research efforts. His present research and publication energies have focused in the areas of youth family problems and alternative forms of non-violent conflict resolution.